Yankee Verse
by
Nathan Marshall Southwick
(1872-1963)

YANKEE VERSE
by
Nathan Marshall Southwick
(1872-1963)

THE WIT AND WISDOM
OF A NEW ENGLAND PHILOSOPHER

Compiled by

Lawrence Southwick

EXPOSITION PRESS
HICKSVILLE, NEW YORK

Appreciation is hereby extended to my wife, Caroline, my brother Thomas, and my sisters Ann and Sarah for their support and encouragement in publishing this book.

—LAWRENCE SOUTHWICK
October 1978

FIRST EDITION

© 1979 by Lawrence Southwick

ISBN 0-682-49205-1

Printed in the United States of America

CONTENTS

ABOUT THE AUTHOR

NATHAN MARSHALL SOUTHWICK
(May 18, 1872-January 13, 1963)

My father, Nathan Marshall Southwick, was born at Maple Hill Farm in Leicester, Massachusetts, on May 18, 1872, the son of Thomas and Ann (Marshall) Southwick. He spent his entire life on this farm, where he died at age ninety in the large colonial house that was built in 1799 by his forebears. The large maple trees lining the approach road for half a mile were set by his father, Thomas, in 1831.

A deed signed by England's King Henry I designating land to Southwick Priory traces the family back to 1100. They emigrated to England from Normandy around 1000. Tradition has it that Lawrence came over on the second voyage of the *Mayflower* in 1627 with William Bradford and other leaders and that his wife and children came over on the third *Mayflower* crossing. They emigrated from Lancashire, England, and settled in Salem, Massachusetts. Lawrence was the colony's first glass manufacturer. His genealogy then proceeded through eight generations: (1) Lawrence, (2) Daniel, (3) Lawrence, (4) Lawrence, (5) Nathaniel, (6) Amasa, (7) Thomas, and (8) Nathan.

Lawrence (1) and Cassandra were persecuted by the Massachusetts Bay Colony for being Quakers and "heretics" and, finally, in their old age, were banished from the colony by Governor Endicott. They went down the coast to Shelter Island on Long Island Sound and died within three days of each other. Their grave in the Sylvester burial lot is inscribed thus:

LAWRENCE AND CASSANDRA SOUTHWICK
Despoiled, imprisoned, starved, whipped, banished
Who fled here to die.

It is noteworthy that the great American poet John Greenleaf Whittier (1807-1892) composed one of his most remarkable poems in 1843 on the event of the auctioning off of a daughter of Lawrence (1), by order of Governor Endicott, to settle certain debts and to satisfy certain heretics. The epic poem is entitled "Cassandra Southwick," but

xiii

the actual person was Provided Southwick, Cassandra's daughter. Fortunately no bids were made.

My father was descended from these strong-willed ancestors and can be described as a New England Yankee, hard-working, persevering, tough. He had finished only a year of high school when, upon the death of his father, he assumed management of the ancestral farm. Nathan Marshall Southwick was a self-made man, who succeeded in the rough and often unruly business worlds of farming, lumbering, farm real estate, and, yes, horsetrading. His interests were legion and included, besides his large family and many friendships, grange, church, politics, sports, farming, fishing, dam building, horses, autos, playing the violin and accordion, checkers, chess, bridge, "magic" tricks, kite flying, writing poetry, and composing songs.

He taught his nine children to be honest and reliant, to farm, to handle guns and traps, to hunt, to cut trees, to run a sawmill, to tap maples, to harvest ice, to load hay, to lay a stone wall, to fish, to swim, to build and fly kites, to play tennis on a homemade farm court, to golf (again on the farm), to skate, to box, to wrestle, to pitch horseshoes, to play chess and checkers, to drive safely, to handle horses, to swing birches, to study, and especially to always work hard and play hard. He abhorred mediocrity and shunned being a "good" loser. The idea was to win in everything. He admonished us to so conduct our lives that we could accomplish anything we set our minds and hands to. We were never to allow ourselves to get "tired," but, if ever we were really tired, we were not to admit it nor let anyone else know it. He also was a practical joker and natural humorist. He liked to sing and recite poetry. He made whistles for his children and grandchildren. He recognized both the serious and the lighter sides of life. He enjoyed life and made many people happy, whether they had known him briefly or as a lifelong friend.

Nathan Marshall Southwick, like his forebears, was a rugged individualist, typical of the traditional New England Yankees who have left their marks on New England and elsewhere by establishing and furthering the basic American standards governing family, neighbor, township, state, and nation. He asked no favors but granted many. A stalwart supporter of honest government, he castigated New Dealism and the budding liberal thinking that fostered the philosophies of what is good for one is good for all, and the government owes everyone a living.

Mr. Southwick never became wealthy in the sense of accumulating money, but he always was healthy in mind and body. Many of his projects and inventions did not pan out. He did extend his basic thinking to his children and friends and by way of his unique verse to a wider following throughout his long and active life. He was called the Bard of Maple Hill and rightly so. He called himself a rhymester. Some of his poetry is serious, much is humorous, and all is typical Americana; all is composed in his inimitable rhyme and meter.

Nathan Marshall Southwick was a product of his time, but, more than many, he also was a producer of his time. He has left a legacy of earnest compassion for effort of brain and brawn. He could not condone laziness and the lack of the will to win. He felt that everyone should try beyond his admitted capacity. This would nurture progress. A thinker and a doer, he left his town and state a better place in which to live.

—LAWRENCE (9) SOUTHWICK
Third Son

PREFACE

When Socrates desired to press his theories on men, in order to assure success, he gave Xenophon the pen. When Shakespeare penned his famous plays, with no one at his side, he little thought each line and phrase would be our future guide. When Einstein added up the score and put his answers down, he knew he'd opened wide the door to science and renown. When Noah Webster made a bet he'd know undying fame, his modern dictionary met the world's profound acclaim. When Whittier's pen delivered ink in never-ending stream, his readers knew just what to think about the slavery scheme. When Izaak Walton wrote his books for angling devotees, he showed the way to bait the hooks to lure the fish with ease, and Samuel Clemens's lively Tom and Huckleberry Finn produced a literary bomb which made the nation grin; so here's a quiet, little tip, before you've read this through, perhaps you'll find a merry quip especially for you!

—NATHAN MARSHALL SOUTHWICK

Yankee Verse
by
Nathan Marshall Southwick
(1872-1963)

ABSURDITIES

I have seen old maids with a pink-rouge blush,
And childless wives with a poodle crush,
But the craziest combination yet
Is a big he-man with a cigarette.

It hangs from his lip with a sickly droop.
A spray of ashes loops the loop,
But he helps to pay the national debt,
This big he-man with a cigarette.

ADVICE (1)

So live that when at last you lie
Beneath the sod piled six feet high,
No man, in truth, can say you erred
Beyond the pale in deed or word.

So live that when at last you go
To join your intimates below,

Or else to greet your friends above,
You'll leave behind a trail of love.

ADVICE (2)

To speak to your own
In frigid tone
Today may engender hate;
So speak to your own
In tender tone;
Tomorrow may be too late.

ALBERTA

A charming young lady, Alberta,
Met a skunk which proceeded to squirt her.
    Billy Bates saw the mess,
    So he helped her undress,
With no notion at all to desert her.

3

Alberta stepped quickly behind him,
Made some passes intending to blind him,
    Stripped the clothes from her guest
    And was speedily dressed,
Leaving Billy as Nature designed him.

ALFALFA

Alfalfa is supposed to be the king of all the plants
That are used for hay and forage on the farm.
But kings are often hard to raise and cannot take a chance
With the elements that tend to do them harm.
And so with King Alfalfa. If we have some fertile land,
Full of lime, and growing not a single weed,
With the right amount of moisture, it will grow to beat the band,
And produce for us a wondrous bunch of feed.
But the trouble with most all New England farming land today
Is the fact it's full of weeds of every kind,
And, unless we use the harrow in a scientific way,
They will leave the frail alfalfa far behind.
But if we labor overtime and give it proper care,
And finally obtain a healthy stand,
It will double up our incomes and the neighbors all will stare
And exclaim, "We wish we owned that kind of land!"

AMOS GRIMES

An aged farmer, Amos Grimes by name,
Supported his emaciated frame
Upon a rustic fence and spoke to Jim,
A little boy who came to talk to him.

Said he, "My days are numbered for this life.
I soon shall quit this unrelenting strife.
I'll kick the bucket, pass in all my chips.
The old grim reaper soon will seal my lips.

"My span of life is coming to an end.
I soon shall bid good-bye to foe and friend.
I'll fly the coop. My race is nearly run.
My earthly tasks are practically done."

The ancient man gazed upward through the air
And sighed, "It won't be long before I'm there."
The boy, with feeling, ventured, "Mr. Grimes,
Do you expect to die so many times?"

ANTIQUES (1)

By use of hammer, saw, and blade
I built a house upon a hill,
Where Nature furnished ample shade
Among the rocks beside a rill,
And when my house was all complete
I toured that section far and wide.
In doing so I hoped to meet
The elders of the countryside.

For deep within those ancient homes
Were many things of bygone days:
Old chairs and bedsteads, musty tomes,
Old bureaus, rockers, chests, and trays.
My quest for antiques netted much
That brought contentment to my mind:
Rare highboys, lowboys, stools and such,
Four-posters, cleverly designed.

I rummaged 'round through attic dust
For things that some would class as trash.
For old-time treasures, red with rust,
And warped and bent I paid my cash.
I hired a jumbo moving van
To take these things to Jones and Weeks,
A firm whose trade announcements ran,
"We Re-condition Rare Antiques."

When from that shop my goods returned
And I had paid a princely price,
I found that I was quite concerned
At daily use of things so nice.
But then the Great Depression came.
My banker sent an urgent call.
I hung my head in grief and shame
To think that I must sell them all.

An antique expert came to town.
I sought him out without delay.
I took him in and brought him down
To price my rare antique display.
He stepped inside and gave one glance,
Then followed up with grunts and groans,
And then remarked, "By any chance,
Did you buy these from Weeks and Jones?"

"Oh, no," I said, "I took them down
For slight repairs." My blood ran cold
As he remarked, "Let's get to town.
They've substituted new for old."
We went. A sign could now be seen
Above the door; they'd moved away.
"Dead Lobsters Red and Live Ones Green,
We Serve Fresh Suckers Every Day."

ANTIQUES (2)

A footstool was my choicest find.
The owner whispered in my ear,
"The legs were cleverly designed
And silver tipped by Paul Revere."

I bought a bedstead that's a fright.
They claimed 'twas used by Lafayette.
He had a nosebleed in the night.
The spots are clearly showing yet.

And there was General Washington,
Who gave us liberty and hope.
I've many chairs he sat upon,
According to the sellers' dope.

I spent my cash at merry clip.
My name became a household thought.
Ben Franklin's kite, Moll Pitcher's slip
Were samples of the things I bought.

The families awaited me;
The members had been deftly coached.
They could not seem to hide their glee
When, bent on purchase, I approached.

The lines above were all complete.
A knock resounded on my door.
I swung it open, there to meet
Some men I'd never seen before.

"We've come to buy your house and land;
Your choice collection, rare and old."
I stuck those guys for forty grand,
And that's the biggest lie I've told.

APPLE TIME

Of course, you remember the sensible saying:
"An apple a day keeps the doctor away."
So why should we flatten our purses by paying
For doctors' prescriptions, our ills to allay?
Ripe apples contain all the nifty nutrition
And qualifications for health that they claim.
Why can't we be blest with enough intuition to
Grasp the advantage by eating the same?

Just think how the members of past generations
Relied upon apples in various ways.
We seem to forget in the world's tribulations
What everyone knew in the earlier days.
But knowledge has given us chance for reflection,
Has furnished us power to decide pro and con,
And those who would shun a ripe apple's protection
In hygienic knowledge is pretty far gone.

With apples so crisp and extremely delicious
'Twould seem that all mothers their virtue should know;
They're wholesome for children and very nutritious.
For elderly people they're malady's foe.
Stewed apples are fine, and baked apples are tasty.
Raw apples bring color and tone to the cheek.
Why fill up your children on pancakes and pastry,
When apples aid greatly their growing physique?

The farmers raise apples to sell to the people.
Expenses are heavy with pruning and spray.
Let's shout once again from some neighborhood steeple:
"An apple a day keeps the doctor away."
Then call up the farmer or visit your grocer;

7

Resolve to buy less that is sealed in a can.
And if he says, "Oranges?" promptly say, "No, sir,
I've come to buy apples, the savior of man."

ARCHIBALD ORR

Old Archibald Orr, by profession a ditcher,
By wielding the shovel grew richer and richer.
To keep in condition, with hammer and wedges
He quarried gray granite from neighboring ledges.

With aid from a scalawag clergyman brother,
He married six widows, one after the other.
They all were desirous of sharing his riches;
Each died and was buried in one of his ditches.

Then, finding no widow, a spinster he wedded,
Bow-legged, sharp-featured, and also red-headed,
With eyes with the knack of not working together,
And skin of the texture of crocodile leather.

This wife got his number as soon as she saw him.
He shelled out the cash when she started to jaw him.
He found very soon, she was wearing the breeches.
He swooned and was buried in one of his ditches.

The Sexton discovered and duly attested
That one of the graves had been lately molested.
The proper officials took charge and asserted
That Archibald's grave appeared strangely deserted.

The red-headed lady with jealousy smarted,
As old Mr. Orr, from his ditch grave, departed,
Was found by the vigilant Constable Liddo,
Asleep on the grave of his favorite widow.

When questioned regarding his chosen location,
Old Archibald grunted a terse explanation,
"A widow is warmer, though death may have met her,
Than any damned spinster of fifty or better."

ARMADILLA SPREE

When the good ship *Armadilla*
Took on water at Antilla,
Certain sailors went ashore to meet the dames,
But they guzzled so much liquor,
Some were sick and others sicker
And the duffers didn't even know their names.

When the time arrived for sailing,
Rules on leave were unavailing.
Not a sailor hit the gangplank with his boot.
So the mate, severely ruffled,
In a voice that wasn't muffled,
Swore he'd smash each blooming culprit on the snoot.

But upon his blunt arrival
At the scene of the revival,
He was asked to take a small Antilla Fizz.
This he downed with satisfaction
And was soon put out of action,
So he couldn't tell which sailing craft was his.

Then the captain, quite courageous,
Said such doings were outrageous
And with grim determination slipped ashore.
He was met by sinful sisters
And was served Antilla Twisters
And was later quite content upon the floor.

So the captain's wife departed.
Said the sisters, open-hearted,
"Won't you take a little nipper just for fun?"
She took one Antilla nipper,
A la sailors, mate, and skipper,
And her search for sailing comrades then was done.

Now aboard the *Armadilla*
In the bay of old Antilla
Were the cook and several sailors fast asleep.
And the wicked cook awoke 'em
By continuing to poke 'em,
Till they landed from their hammocks in a heap.

Then with torrid exhortation
He gave out the information
That, as captain, he was bound to sail the seas.

9

They unfurled the sails and spanker,
    Manned the wheel and weighed the anchor,
And skedaddled on the tropic summer breeze.

    Sailing onward through the billows,
    They espied some waving willows
On the sweetest little island ever seen.
    Through their telescopic glasses,
    They could see a flock of lassies
Flitting nimbly through the forest, dark and green.

    Being men of virile vision,
    They uncorked a quick decision
And proceeded to enact it with a smile.
    Heaving to, they made a landing
    And obtained an understanding
With the ladies who took refuge on the isle.

    Expert swimmers, daring divers,
    These young ladies, sole survivors
Of a shipwreck, quite some time ago, they said,
    After swimming saw a highland,
    Which turned out to be the island,
Where they were and they were willing to be wed.

    They forsook the *Armadilla*
    And built up a charming villa
On that lovely spot encircled by the sea.
    And for centuries thereafter
    Could be heard the ringing laughter
Of descendants of the *Armadilla* spree.

ARTIST

A little brush, a little toil,
    An easel and a stool,
A little pigment mixed with oil,
    A canvas and a rule,
A final touch, his labors cease;
    He lays it by to dry.
And there is born a masterpiece
    That no one cares to buy.

Chagrined, he stoops to vulgar trash,
    Surrealistic mush.
The daub, the splotch, the splash, the dash
    Are alien to his brush,
But plaudits from the hoi polloi
    Alleviate the strain.
He can't repress a tinge of joy,
    For now he eats again.

AT LAST

My rhyming days are on the blink.
    I find I'm no repeater.
Time was when I was in the pink
    At rhythm, rhyme, and meter.

Time was when I could rhyme a word,
    Two syllables or single,
But now my rhyming sounds absurd,
    And lacks the jolly jingle.

It's unromantic to confess
    I've lost the rhyming magic.
I might have reaped renowned success,
    But now my plight is tragic.

Henceforth I'll cling to sordid prose
    In stating thought and action.
That's quite a drop from pride that goes
    With rhyming satisfaction.

AT THE RACES

It was not too long ago when I met Eliza Lowe
    At the races where your money fades away.
She was really out of luck when she bet her final buck
    On the dapple gray instead of on the bay.
"I am broke," she sadly said, as she coyly hung her head
    With her golden tresses waving in the breeze.
So I humbly volunteered, as the shades of night appeared,
    To escort her on a ramble 'neath the trees.

11

The moon had gone to rest in its cradle in the west,
    With the grass as soft as velvet in the park;
And I'll now confide to you, though you'll scarce believe it true,
    We were picking four-leafed clovers in the dark.

Though I searched among the grass with that interesting lass,
    Four-leafed clovers seemed extremely hard to find.
As I took an upward glance, those elusive four-leafed plants
    Were becoming less attractive to my mind.
But the time must always end when communing with a friend,
    And I knew she'd lost her last remaining dime;
So I slipped her ample dough for wherever she might go,
    Till I'd meet her somewhere else some other time.

The moon had gone to rest in its cradle in the west,
    With the grass as soft as velvet in the park;
And I'll still confide to you, though you'll scarce believe it true,
    We were picking four-leafed clovers in the dark.

AT YEAR'S END

There is something very precious which is coming to us all;
So let everyone be ready to receive the welcome call.
We shall hear it in the valley, on the mountaintop and plain,
From the Bay of San Francisco to the pine-clad slopes of Maine.

It's a thing we all may cherish with devotion and esteem.
It's a priceless gift of nature. It is not an idle dream.
That there's no misunderstanding, let us make the message clear;
This donation we're receiving is a glorious brand-New Year.

ATONEMENT

Still was the night; the heart was stiller still,
Which served its purpose well in time gone by.
The moon's pale beams spread light upon the hill,
Where fate decreed the victim fall and die
By the assassin's hand. The fatal blow
Was struck, though malice entered not therein,
And yet it may be difficult to show
That such an act was not a cardinal sin.

However, valid reason must admit
That taking life should never be condoned,
And man, who violates the Holy Writ,
Should state just why his act should be atoned.

But here we need no vindicating plea;
He put to death a living Christmas tree.

AURORA BOREALIS

No human hand could have the magic touch
To paint upon an artist's canvas such
A masterpiece as oft appears on high,
Aurora Borealis in the sky.

The Author of a work so vast and grand
Depicts a gorgeous scene, divinely planned.
With magic brush, celestially He spreads
Resplendent purples, greens and grays and reds.

We mortals gaze upon Aurora's light,
Displayed in brilliant streamers through the night,
And marvel at the varying shades of chrome
That only God can spread on Heaven's dome.

THE AUTOMOBILE

They say the automobile game has barely started yet.
It's only in its infancy, a playful little pet.
But if it grows for twenty years the way that it has grown
Throughout the twenty years just passed, 'twill surely walk alone.

The early automobile furnished blessings by the score.
It gave a lot of people work who never'd worked before.
They'd crank and crank and clean the plugs, and fix the speed control,
Until they looked as if they'd been for weeks a-heaving coal.

It put their clothes upon the bum. The tailor jobs were fine,
And male attendance at the churches showed a sharp decline.
And conversation grew a-pace until the common man
Could scarcely understand at all the automobile fan.

13

But then with swift rapidity great changes came in view.
The cars of single cylinder were now equipped with two.
In place of starting with a jump, they'd hop along instead.
They made just twice the noise while backing up or going ahead.

Instead of sprocket chains, they used big driving gears of steel.
The rudder was abandoned for the modern steering wheel.
The engine underneath was placed, instead of in the rear.
The gas and smoke from burning oil would through the floor appear,

Enabling every one on board to heave a joyful sigh,
By showing them the gas and oil were still in good supply.
But greater changes still were due. The monster touring "four"
Appeared upon our highways with a rumble and a roar.

The makers still were going ahead, and so the engine placed
Away up front, where troubles could more easily be traced.
The modern "four" soon opened up a field so vast and wide
That everyone who had the price must in an auto ride.

The farmers all must have them, so that they might ride to town,
And do their business quicker and thus keep expenses down.
And city folks must have them, thus enabling the charms
Of country life to come to them from contact with the farms.

The change was fine for everyone, and everything went well,
Until the farmers found they didn't have so much to sell.
The city folks would ramble out and steal their fowl and crops,
Then speed away and soon roll in among the silent cops.

The farmers vowed they'd catch the thieves, or else the reason know.
The city folks made up their minds the "four" was far too slow,
And so the sixes and the eights and then the twelves appeared.
So now the safest crop the farmer raises is his beard.

With the moral of this little rhyme the farmer is concerned.
He can't reduce the cylinders. Their value has been learned.
But with a hundred cylinders no automobile flier
Can ramble very swiftly with a bullet in a tire.

AUTOMOBILE MECHANIC

Why curse and condemn the poor auto mechanic,
Who labors so hard in the grease and the grime?
Why work ourselves into a pulsating panic,

14

Because he can't finish our auto on time?
We knew very well when we placed in his keeping
Our choice limousine for adjustments and such,
That his unfailing fault was his weakness for sleeping,
While busily testing the camshaft or clutch.

The auto mechanic has reason for pity,
For everyone calls him a sluggard and shirk.
He'll sing us a song or an up-to-date ditty
To keep our attention away from his work.
He fusses around with the chisel and hammer,
When all that he needs are the pliers and wrench.
We mustn't grow nervous and broadcast a clamor,
Till forty-five trips he has made to his bench.

The auto mechanic, of course, has his trials,
For instance, at times when he seeks to dispense
The same grade of oil in three shiny quart vials,
One fifteen, one twenty, one twenty-five cents.
He sends in his bill for just ninety-six dollars
For peeking around under Mr. Smith's hood,
But Smith doesn't pay, so he bellows and hollers
And settles for twenty; that's ten to the good.

Mechanics there are who are honestly dealing
And building up trade that is making them rich.
For such men as these we have kindest of feeling
And stop every time that our cars get the itch.
However, when told that our bulbs are all sprouted
And, what is much worse, our compression is bent,
We cannot be blamed, if their motives we've doubted,
For fleeing before other ills they invent.

BANKER

There's a soft-spoken, handsome young man in our town.
His name, you recall, is Theophilus Brown.
Among weak-minded people he's gained some renown,
    This soft-spoken, handsome young man.

He wears a bow tie; his complexion is fair,
And toward his left eyebrow he parts his brown hair.
He skips here and there like a thing made of air,
    This soft-spoken, handsome young man.

He's the head of our local cooperative bank,
A large institution of excellent rank,
For which our community glumly may thank
    This soft-spoken, handsome young man.

They publish their ads in alluring display.
"Come in, and we'll show you our wizardly way."
They're most reassuring, the things he will say,
    This soft-spoken, handsome young man.

"We'll furnish you cash, for a home all your own.
Just pick out a site in a certified zone.
Now sign on the line and we'll make you a loan,"
    Says this soft-spoken, handsome young man.

"Now keep up your payments and all will be nice.
Just follow our plans and our valued advice.
Of course, we do this at a nominal price,"
    Says this soft-spoken, handsome young man.

The home is now built and the victim moves in.
The overhead starts and the payments begin.
"With barrels of luck you are certain to win,"
    Says this soft-spoken, handsome young man.

But now the mills stop and the income is nil.
Each month brings along a cooperative bill.
"I'm sorry, but you've obligations to fill,"
    Says this soft-spoken, handsome young man.

The wife is despondent, the children in tears,
As slowly but surely ejection day nears.
"Be quick. Make it snappy. You're clogging the gears,"
    Says this soft-spoken, handsome young man.

"Come on, little homestead; come under my wing.
Hard luck with no pay is a terrible thing.
But death has, by far, a more vigorous sting,"
    Says this soft-spoken, handsome young man.

The incident closed, we will add up the score.
He paid and he lost, for he couldn't pay more.
"I've noticed the fact there are suckers galore,"
    Says this soft-spoken, handsome young man.

New ads now appear in a customer quest.
"We've five hundred thousand we wish to invest.
Come in and see us and then feather your nest,"
    Says this soft-spoken, handsome young man.

And so, once again, a new bunch of gazooks
Will start paying cash to a rabble of rooks.
But some time or other they'll put up their dukes
　　To this soft-spoken, handsome young man.

"Now that is the way that the law used to be.
Times change, and the companies now must agree
To give back your money, deducting their fee,"
　　Says this soft-spoken, handsome young man.

So when you apply for a loan, keep in mind
There isn't a catch in the note you have signed.
Believe it or not, a true friend you will find
　　In this soft-spoken, handsome young man.

BASEBALL BET

I sat one sunny afternoon upon a grandstand seat.
The local ball team tried right hard, the out-of-towns to beat.
The game was fast; the visitors had gathered quite a lead.
But still the locals had a chance, if they could show more speed.
Not far from me a small boy sat. Big tears were in his eyes.
I watched him closely for a while. Then something made me rise.
I tiptoed over where he sat, and, leaning low, said I,
"A ballgame is a funny place for little boys to cry."
He looked at me and then replied, "It wouldn't make you gay,
If you went home and found your mother'd gone away to stay.
You see, it's just like this," he said. "Before my ma and pa
Were married, Mr. Arthur Jones was courting my mamma.
And when he couldn't marry her, it made him awful sore.
He went away and didn't come around here anymore.
But just last night our door-bell rang and Mr. Jones walked in.
He gave mamma a funny look, which made my papa grin.
They all shook hands, and then sat down and chinned to beat the band.
They talked about a lot of things I couldn't understand.
Then papa said to Mr. Jones, 'We have our final game
Between our local ball team and the nine from Notre Dame;
So meet me at the baseball grounds tomorrow afternoon.
I'll bet our boys will trim that bunch, and sing the victory tune!'
'How much you bet?' asked Mr. Jones. 'I'll take a chance on that.'
'Oh! Anything you wish,' said my papa right off the bat.
And so you see," my young friend said (his voice was all ajar),
"If Mr. Jones should win that bet, of course, he'll take mamma."

Just then ten thousand shouts were heard. My little friend and I
Looked down upon that diamond, beneath a cloudless sky.
A home run by some local boy brought three more runs around.
Our team had won. That boy's mamma for him was safe and sound.

BATHTUBS

I shall never forget, though the years slowly flow,
The first bathtub we had forty-five years ago.
What bathing we did, altho now it seems strange,
Was done in a tub by the old kitchen range.

The plumber came up with his piping and tools
And fashioned our bathroom according to rules.
Both hot and cold water equipment, and such,
Went into that bathroom we needed so much.

That evening my mother was first to jump in.
Then dad took his turn with a satisfied grin.
And dad was a man of great waistband and weight;
Two hundred and thirty I safely can state.

He turned the hot faucet and stepped in the tub,
Then slipped and sat down with a rub-a-dub-dub.
The water kept coming; steam rose in a cloud.
And dad could be heard meditating aloud.

The adjectives came in a thunderous stream;
The nouns, verbs, and adverbs were muffled in steam.
He put them together and broadcast a yell,
"Gorram it; this water is hotter than anything!"

I pulled on the door which was fastened inside,
As dad gave a roar he was losing his hide.
The steam was escaping through crevice and crack,
As dad made his lunges, but always fell back.

His tummy was shaped like a forty-inch ball;
To reach to that faucet he couldn't, that's all.
The water streamed in like a gusher of oil,
And father continued to bellow and boil.

At last, with a desperate wrench and a yank,
The lock broke away with a clash and a clank,
And there I could see in the midst of his woes
Dad trying to shut off the stream with his toes.

18

With hot water splashing all over the place,
I knew my dear daddy was not saying grace.
I stopped the hot water and turned on the cold,
Because that's exactly what I had been told.

I laughed till I cried and was losing my breath,
But now my dear daddy was freezing to death.
That icy cold water produced quite a change.
The fact that he felt it was not at all strange.

I pulled up the plug and the water ran out,
And dad was excited without any doubt.
He shivered and shook as he lay there and moaned,
So I helped him ashore while he grunted and groaned.

By rubbing him well he was partly consoled,
And, believe it or not, sir, he didn't catch cold.
As he lay in his bed, snugly tucked as could be,
He whispered these words, "No more bathtubs for me."

BEAR FACTS

When I came back from overseas and quit the bloomin' army,
I planned to lead a life of ease so went to Alabamy.
The people there are native sons; no use have they for slackers.
The population mostly runs to mountaineers and crackers.

And so I thought 'twould be a spot well suited to my wishes.
I'd hunt a bear as like as not and mingle with the fishes.
I'd heard the bears were round about within the mountain passes,
And all required to drive them out were mountain lads and lassies.

And so I made my weary way to land of moonshine whiskey.
I didn't know a soldier jay would find it rather risky.
But on a peak ten thousand feet above the ocean level,
A shot rang out with echo neat, which scared me like the devil.

I could not tell from whence it came. No motion met my vision.
I saw at once the mountain game required a quick decision.
The armistice I reproduced in mighty clever fashion,
And then a call I quickly loosed denoting lack of passion.

"A friend," I wailed in accents mild and shot both arms above me.
I hoped 'twould make them reconciled to spare my life and love me.
And then I saw three lanky guys equipped with shooting irons
Of proper length and weight and size for bagging mountain lions.

"A friend," I said. "I wish you well. I like your noble features.
I wish to stay with you a spell and hunt the mountain creatures.
I have a scheme to catch a bear; it's clever, sure, and classy.
'Twill disengage him from his lair, although he's sour and sassy."

You should have seen those mountaineers stroll down in my direction.
The razor blade for years and years had vanished from that section.
"There's just one thing we do with spies," said one old bloke named
    Stratton.
"We strings 'em upward toward the skies and perforates their pattern."

"I'm not a spy," I quickly said. "I lately came from Flanders.
I'm sick of hearing screaming lead. I'm full of chills and janders.
I simply wish to hunt a bear upon this reservation,
Provided that you do not care and give your approbation."

Those moonshine makers viewed me long. I stood with breath abated.
They'd surely shoot me for a song. I don't know why they waited,
But something told them I was dumb and one by one they wilted.
And then they motioned me to come and soon a chair I tilted.

The house was neither large nor small, but cozy as a palace.
All kinds of furs adorned the wall. The daughter's name was Alice,
A peachy girl of seventeen. I'll say she was a keener.
Oh, boy, but what a movie queen she'd make at Pasadena.

Well, everything is rolling fine; bear steak adorns the platter.
Then comes the Mountain Dew and wine and then to bed we scatter.
But when the morning sun appears I ramble to the kitchen
To see that girl of tender years. Oh, gosh, but she's bewitchin'.

I wises up this lass sublime about my mountain mission.
I tell her I shall spend my time a-huntin' bears and fishin',
And then I spring the latest dope. (Of course, she thinks it's funny.)
In catching bears I use a rope and just a pail of honey.

Just then old Stratton rambles in and hears my explanation.
He downs a quart of Mountain Gin and wants a demonstration.
So after breakfast out we go to where the bears are snoozing.
We see their tracks upon the snow, so all looks quite enthusing.

The noose we place upon a mound, the honey pail inside it.
The rope we stretch upon the ground. With snow we deftly hide it,
And down the gulch we tie it fast around a mountain popple.
And now we're all prepared at last to see a bruin topple.

Then all of us ascend some trees and in their branches nestle,
So everyone can plainly see the bear with honey wrestle.
When all is quiet and serene, not long we have to dally.
A monstrous bear is plainly seen approaching from the valley.

He ambles up at record speed. He sniffs the sweet aroma.
You'd think he hadn't had a feed since leaving Oklahoma,
For straightway to that honey pail he makes his way a-crashing.
From side to side he wags his tail; his jaws are loudly gnashing.

But now we notice down the glen another bear advances,
And I can see those stalwart men exchanging furtive glances.
And now we see another bear, and now we see another.
They seem to come from everywhere. They're following their mother.

But, holy smoke! they're coming still in pairs and fours and dozens.
And swiftly scrambling up the hill, come uncles, aunts, and cousins.
We're up against a hopeless task. The bears are coming thicker.
Old Lanky Stratton draws a flask and takes a swig of liquor.

I then perceive the other guys have followed dad's example.
Each draws a flask of wondrous size and takes a goodly sample.
And then each takes a glance at me and then at one another.
A rifle rests upon each knee. I long for home and mother.

It's plain to see those mountaineers have set their brains to thinking.
They're drowning now their deadly fears by constant spells of drinking.
The thoughts within their muddled brains are soon to be broadcasted.
My bear enthusiasm wanes; my joys and hopes are blasted.

Old Lanky sits astride a limb. His feet are now in motion.
The bears are surging under him like billows on the ocean.
And now and then they glance aloft and see his legs a-waving.
His outlook sure is far from soft. He's on the point of caving.

And now the others swing their legs; they saw their dad begin it.
Their flasks are emptied to the dregs; they're drunker every minute.
The bears begin to congregate beneath the swinging members.
Their little eyes pour forth their hate from tiny burning embers.

Now old man Stratton looks at me and cocks his bloomin' rifle.
I slides around behind the tree; I simply move a trifle.
I now am clearly out of sight from all those drunken bruisers.
I have to cling with all my might, but beggars can't be choosers.

The bears perceive my motion slight, and amble down beneath me.
They seem prepared to stay all night to torture or to teeth me.
But now old Stratton yells aloud, "Get ready, boys, and shoot him.
He wanted bears and this here crowd is pretty sure to suit him."

But now I pulls a nifty trick. I grabs my tam-o'-shanter
And hangs it on a little stick and shoves it out for banter.
Three rifle cracks then greet my ears and down the old hat topples,
And I can hear three lusty cheers from out those mountain popples.

21

They think they've made me bite the dust. The bears are surging hither.
Old Stratton yells, "It's home or bust." And down the trees they slither.
And down the hill they strike such gaits, no antelope could match 'em;
And all the bears in seven states would have no chance to catch 'em.

I prophesied my time was short; a sudden slip would end it.
The bears around my tree would snort and then take turns to tend it.
For just two days and just two nights they kept me in my prison.
The wind pursued me dead to rights, and I was nearly frizen.

The morning of the third arrived. The breeze was growing rougher.
Of food and drink I'd been deprived so long, I'd ceased to suffer.
I gazed beneath but not a bear appeared within the section.
I looked around me everywhere and figured on direction.

Old Stratton and the boys had flown along the streamlet's trickle.
I felt my chances all alone to be extremely fickle.
But surely I could get a drink and something have inside me,
Assisting me to clearly think of certain signs to guide me.

As on that poplar limb I sit, my mind to Alice wanders,
And when a fellow's heart is hit he lingers not, nor ponders.
I slip my legs around the trunk with painful tribulation.
I feel like I'd been on a drunk of fourteen weeks' duration.

At last upon the ground I stand. My legs are weak and wobble.
The pains shoot round to beat the band. At first I scarcely hobble.
Perchance a bear comes on the scene, he'd find I lacked ambition.
I couldn't shin a lima bean to save me from perdition.

But, thank my stars, the bears are gone. I totter toward the timber.
Though I am weary, weak, and wan, my legs are growing limber.
I limply kneel upon the brink beside the sparkling water,
And place with that life-saving drink the moonshine-maker's daughter.

Although I'd roosted on that limb until my eyes were glassy,
No moment found my memory dim in dreaming of that lassie.
I'd never met a winsome maid of such enticing features.
She'd place in dark and dismal shade all painted female creatures.

No mountain bears nor mountain men could circumvent our meeting.
And so I started down the glen for time was swiftly fleeting.
I traveled on for quite a spell; surroundings looked familiar,
And then I heard a fearful yell, "Come here, Pa. Come here; will ya?"

I quickly stepped in plainest view and saw the cabin, cozy.
Old Stratton took a step or two; things didn't look so rosy.
I made no move as aim he took. I sensed a long vacation.
A "click." That's all. He wore a look of utter consternation.

His faithful rifle failed to fire. I quickly strode beside him.
To punch his nose I'd great desire, but simply deigned to chide him.
"That's four times, now, you've done your best to punctuate my liver;
And just four times you've been outguessed." His frame began to quiver.

"From me, you nothing have to fear, if calm you'll be and quiet,
But bullets whizzing by my ear are bad for steady diet.
You're just a playful, little elf, unless I am mistaken;
And now I'd like to wrap myself around a slab of bacon."

A tiny finger motioned me within the cozy kitchen,
And soon the bacon joyously was curlin' and a-twitchin'.
And as I watched that form sublime move swiftly yon and hither,
My thoughts rolled backward to a time that fairly made me wither.

That time, I gently fell in love and nearly had a wedding.
She filled me up with turtle dove while toward the altar heading.
I thought I loved my Hazel Eyes and plastered her with kisses,
Then someone kindly put me wise: already she was Mrs.

And that was when I took the train and joined the army forces.
I never passed that way again; I'm leery of divorces,
But all such thoughts were now dispelled. I'd something for my money.
The maiden that I here beheld was pure as clover honey.

She placed my plate, and, leaning low, within my ear drum, eager,
Deposited sufficient woe to stun a Texas leaguer.
"I cannot go away," I said. "I cannot leave you, dearie.
I dodged the Germans' red-hot lead, emerging bright and cheery."

"But Dad's a man," she whispered back, "who gives or takes no quarter.
I can't leave Daddy, Jim, and Jack, for I'm the only daughter.
I pulled the charge from Daddy's gat. I knew you'd be returning."
She gave my hand a little pat; oh, gosh, my heart was burning.

I glanced without; the boys and dad were grimly talking turkey,
With often from the taller lad gesticulations jerky.
I ate the meal that angel made and then, to fill the docket,
A lightning shave with safety blade I carried in my pocket.

And then I pulled a crazy act, but simply did my duty.
And, though it surely wisdom lacked, I kissed that writhing beauty.
It was a long and lingering kiss, I'll tell you, gentle reader,
The kind that ends in joy and bliss, a perfect sweetheart breeder.

Then, after that, I could have met a thousand gray gorillas.
I stepped outside and swore to get those mountaineer distillers.
I placed my hand upon my hip and said to Mr. Stratton,
"The time has come, unless I slip, to perforate your pattern."

"Now, just a moment," he replied. "You're quite a decent feller.
We haven't found within your hide a single streak of yeller.
Suppose we shake and call it quits. Ye've surely earned yer bacon.
We tried to shoot ye into bits, but found we were mistaken."

I stood there camouflaged in calm, until his words digested,
And then within that massive palm my trembling fingers nested.
I'd never felt a firmer grip; my arm was twisted roughly.
My other hand was on my hip as Stratton murmured gruffly,

"We'll lay the guns here, side by side, to show there'll be no roughing."
"I have no gun," I then replied. "I'm quite a hand at bluffing."
"By hell," Old Stratton meekly spoke; his face was drawn and ashen.
"Is this another Yankee joke ye've pulled in clever fashion?"

"We shook," said I, "to always bar the gunplay; let's not break it.
I'll sell the moonshine faster, far, than all of us can make it."
Old Stratton scratched his withered dome and said, "It's time fer matin'.
Go in and make yerself ter home; the daughter's likely waitin'."

At present I'm established in producing Moonshine Merry.
We specialize in Jackall Gin and Bear Ridge Cherry Sherry.
So now, my friends, just write to me at Alabama Border,
And P.D.Q. and C.O.D. we'll ship it to your order.

THE BEGGAR

Unkempt, unshaven, and unshod,
A pearly tear bedimmed his eye,
As dimes and nickels, gifts from God,
Dropped in his cup by passersby.

Rejoiced, as duskiness appeared,
He sought the shadows as a screen,
Put on his shoes, removed his beard,
And vanished in his limousine.

BILLY WILKINS
HITS THE BALL

CLAY COUNTY twilight leaguers had assembled for the fray.
From the starting of the season CLAY and LYME had led the way.
Both the grandstand and the bleachers were congested to the beams
With the throng of royal rooters who with pride had backed their teams.

As the players took their places and the ball went shooting 'round,
Deafening shouts of wild approval made a grand, tumultuous sound.
Belts were tightened; bats were waving as they dusted off the plate.
Twenty thousand fans were waiting for the magic touch of fate.

CLAY and LYME were tied for honors with percentage eighty-four.
Every fan was clearly conscious that this game could change the score,
And the winners well deserving of their manager's esteem
Would be hailed as conquering heroes by the rooters for their team.
With the batteries selected and the umpires waiting there,
As the pitcher got the signal there was tenseness in the air.
Well they knew those rival pitchers with their magic curves and speed
Made a hit by any player very difficult indeed.

One by one the curving zippers sank within the catcher's mitt.
One by one those wizard batters fanned the air and threw a fit.
One by one the innings vanished and each goose egg took its place
Till the ninth had been completed. Not a man had reached first base.
Such a perfect pitcher's battle rooters never saw in play.
Clever signals, airtight twirling, were the features of the day.
Though the umpires feared the gloaming, they were loath to call the
    game.
They allowed another inning. Could not someone bid for fame?

One, two, three, the LYMES went hitless, then the home team
    came to bat;
As the ball came hurtling toward him, Billy swung and hit it flat.
Just above the short third baseman sailed the ball at dazzling speed.
Billy legged it down the baseline. Just one run would clinch the lead.
Rounding first he raced for second with a true Bill Wilkins stride,
Touched the base and sprinted forward as the throw was high and wide.
Third was near. The ball sped onward. Baseman fumbled; light was dim.
But the tall and lanky shortstop scooped it as it rolled to him.

With a lightning throw to catcher they'd defeat a certain win,
If perchance the catcher caught it, tagging Billy coming in.
Fate was fickle; luck was lacking. Catcher reached a bit too late,
Dropped the ball, and Billy Wilkins slid across the old home plate.
From the grandstand came a warhoop, from the bleachers cheer on cheer.
What a fitting demonstration for the climax of the year.
Hats were flying; yelling thousands swelled the wild, triumphant howl,
While on third the grinning baseman heard an umpire bellow, "FOUL."

Down upon the field in thousands surged a throng of frenzied fans
With a grim determination to fulfill their chosen plans.
"Kill him; kill him," came in chorus with the echoes from the stands,
But the umpire had departed with dispatch to other lands.

Many fans declared the ball was fair, but some did not agree
And claimed it was too dark out there for anyone to see.
But should that umpire come around at any distant day,
He'd get a hot reception from the baseball fans at CLAY.

That play will be debated pro and con till Kingdom come.
And that umpire will be classified a hero or a bum.
It's well to stop a baseball game unless there's ample light.
A well-established precedent—The umpire's always right.
We do not dare to criticize. The umpire's word is law.
Although we're very certain that his acts are rank and raw.
He occupies a gilded throne. It's useless to rebel.
Although we think he's biased and incompetent as anything.

BLACKSTONE RIVER

Years have come and years have gone, and the world
Goes gaily on. Long ago I swapped old dobbin for a
Flivver, but my mind goes rambling back to the dear
Old slabwood shack, where we camped upon the roaring
Blackstone River.

Oh, the merry times I had, as a freckled, barefoot
Lad, and the recollections fairly make me quiver.
We felt glum and out of luck, if we failed to stalk
A buck in the marshes of the foaming
Blackstone River.

There we used to slowly float in the old flat-bottomed
Boat with our fishlines hanging down for perch or
Kiver. I still hear my comrades shout, as we yanked
The gamey pout from the waters of the tepid
Blackstone River.

Oh, my thoughts will ne'er grow dim, how we'd splash
And dive and swim, and then stand around upon the bank
And shiver; then with fast-increasing wrath, we'd go
Home and take a bath, after bathing in our cherished
Blackstone River.

But we wish that we might be once again upon one knee
Kindling fires to fry our bacon, fish, or liver. As
We at the future gaze, we see no such joyous days like
The ones we spent so well on the beauteous
Blackstone River.

BOATING

Daddy and Junior were fishing for pout
    Late in the afternoon.
Along came a hurricane, dumping them out.
    Odd for the month of June.

Helplessly Junior sank lower and lower,
    Floundering around like a clown.
Daddy could swim so he hastened ashore,
    Just as the son went down.

BOOTHE

Old Alexander Barney Boothe
Was never known to tell the truth.
His grave is on Ascension Hill.
We wonder if he's lying still.

THE BOWERY

'Twas on the Bowery late one night, a sailor, worse for liquor,
Decided he would have a bite, where tungstens flare and flicker.
He strolled within a neat café. His gait was quite amusing.
A seat he took, and there, they say, the waitress found him snoozing.

"What shall it be?" the waitress said. The man of vision bleary
Replied, with senses semi-dead, "What shall it be? Yes, dearie."
"A lovely salad I will bring," she chirped. " 'Twill make you happy."
"A lovely salad. That's the thing, and, dearie, make it snappy."

The salad came. The drowsy guy another nap was taking.
She left the salad where his eye would see it, on awaking.
In course of time the dreamy maze departed from the fellow.
He yawned and fixed his burning gaze upon the salad yellow.

With trembling hand the fork he gripped. His purpose was inspection.
The salad stirred and slid and slipped in every known direction.
"Come, dearie, come. Come here to me." The waitress sauntered over.
"A gentleman I am," said he, "altho I'm quite a rover;

"But now a question I shall raise. This thing has got me guessing."
"What is it?" asked the waiting girl, for time was sorely pressing.
Said he, "Altho I must allow I'm fairly full of red-eye,
This question I will ask you now: Do I eat that, or did I?"

BRAIN VERSUS BRAWN

The time has come when most of us should take an inventory.
The virtue of the blunderbuss is now an ancient story.
Though once it was a weapon, grand, its usefulness is banished.
And many other things we've canned, because their worth has vanished.
The wondrous stage coach in the race with trains and autos speedy
Would now appear quite out of place and look extremely seedy.
The ancient ways of doing stunts have now been superseded
By modern methods, which at once the world has quickly heeded.
I don't suppose a change has come that's caused such ardent boosters
And made the wheels of fortune hum like breeding hens and roosters.
The old-time ways have gone to pot upon the poultry question.
For modern fowls, as like as not, they'd furnish indigestion.
Our methods now are far ahead of anything before us.
For proof of this within the shed we hear a joyful chorus.
It's all because we've learned the trick to feed a balanced ration
And thus produce from every chick the eggs to feed the nation.
No harder 'tis to feed the flocks the proper sort of fodder,
Than cramming stuff through Plymouth Rocks digestible as solder.
And food for prize Ancona fowls, producing no reaction,
Brings naught from them but dismal howls of rank dissatisfaction.
The man who studies long and hard, variety and measure,
Can gaze within his chicken yard with fast-increasing pleasure,
While he who simply chucks the swill inside the hen enclosure
Can ne'er expect to climb the hill within a classy Lozier.
It's just the time to buy right now a thousand or a dozen.
So talk it over with your frau, your uncle, or your cousin.
Just whisper to the girls and boys that chickens are the berries.
Start in at once and reap the joys and mingle with the merries.
The prolific *Poultry Journal* man will steer you o'er the eddies.
'Twill make of you a loyal fan for buffs or whites or reddies.
And when your fortune you have made with brain instead of muscle
You'll sit at Palm Beach in the shade and watch the land sharks hustle.

THE BROOK

The poet chronicles my source,
    As swampland that I'm leaving
With gentle haste, but gathering force,
    As in and out I'm weaving.

The quail and thrush have been my friends,
    Since first I started flowing
Down hill and dale, around the bends,
    By pastureland and mowing.

As slowly through the reedy vale
    Descends my placid water,
I hear the whistle of the quail;
    I feel the plunging otter.

'Neath forest shade I babble on
    (According to the poet)
O'er rocky ledge and out upon
    The pebbled sands below it.

Now, when the poet penned his lines,
    He knew what he was doing.
I DID cavort beneath the pines,
    My pleasant way pursuing.

I DID meander, now and then,
    Beneath the rustic bridges,
Or glide beside the beaver's den
    Between the rocky ridges.

But now the march of progress takes
    Its toll from nature's beauty.
The brain of modern mankind makes
    Advance a bounden duty.

The woodsmen fell the giant trees
    That long were my salvation,
And sawmills fashion boards from these
    For modern habitation.

Huge shovels disarrange my shale
    And rip my banks to pieces.
Through ditches in my marshy swale
    My life-blood ebbs, then ceases.

Man's plows and harrows rake my bed
    Where lately I was flowing,
And one may hear the farmer's tread
    Where garden plots are growing.

No more the timid frog and tern
    May with my brook trout wrestle.
No more beneath my reed and fern
    The snipe and partridge nestle.

My time has come. I've lost the race.
    I made my best endeavor.
The march of progress takes my place,
    And I am gone forever.

BUMBLEBEE

The bumblebee is blithe and gay,
And toils from morn till night.
He mixes up his work and play
Within the petals bright.

He hustles 'round from flower to flower
And spreads the germ of life,
And seldom has an idle hour
To frolic with his wife.

While out upon his daily grind,
If he should bothered be,
His bold attack is from behind,
A stern reality.

He dresses up in gorgeous gown
In colors bright and gay.
He looks as pretty upside down
As any other way.

THE BUTTERNUT TREE

There stands by a wall on our farm on the hill
A butternut tree that I reverence still,
For beneath its broad branches that waved to and fro
I talked to a lass thirty-nine years ago.

30

Her age was sixteen and her charms far outshone
The ones that adorned any girl I had known.
And many rash thoughts were engendered in me,
As we talked in the shade of that butternut tree.

She mentioned that college would come in the fall
And said that Mount Holyoke had answered her call.
My brain felt a thrill when she hastened to say,
"Mount Holyoke is scarce forty-nine miles away."

I spoke of the college's culture and charm;
She spoke of the marvelous life on a farm.
But we found many topics on which to agree,
While sharing the shade of that butternut tree.

The college course ended. She then was of age.
I figured my knowledge as that of a sage.
For years I had known what my sentiments were,
But managed to keep them a secret from her.

I opened my heart to that princess divine.
She nestled so closely I knew she was mine.
And our nine darling kiddies have sprung from my knee
To play in the shade of that butternut tree.

BY THE RIVER

'Twas down by the river I met her one day.
As she was alone I decided to stay.
Her bathing suit clung in an intimate way,
    And I found myself falling in love.
    "I beg pardon," I purred,
    Held my breath for an answering word.
"My Dad owns the bank in this town," she averred,
    And I knew I had fallen in love.

    Oh, how fanciful love can be
    With your feelings a-quiver;
    That is the way that it came to me
    Down on the bank of the river.

She changed to her clothes in the bushes nearby,
Which took her so long that I thought I should die.
But when she appeared, what a treat to the eye.
    No wonder I'd fallen in love.

Oh, what exquisite grace,
Frills of satin and lace,
And I knew by the glow on her radiant face
That the lady had fallen in love.

Just the two of us, there we were,
With our feelings a-quiver.
Love had suddenly come to her
Down on the bank of the river.

CALEB CASE

Old Caleb Case, a wealthy man,
    Alert and on the square,
Was sitting on his porch one day,
    Partaking of the air.
He'd lost his wife the year before
    And since had lived alone.
His reverie was shattered as
    He heard the telephone.

The voice was mild, "Oh, Mr. Case,
    We'd like to call on you.
We're seeking homes for refugees;
    Could you take in a few?
We hope you're able, Mr. Case.
    We're open now for bids.
We'll have expectant mothers and,
    Of course, there'll be the kids."

Old Caleb paused a moment then
    And calmly scratched his head.
He drew a breath of mountain air
    And seriously said,
"I'll take expectant mothers as
    The members of my fold.
Don't have them too expectant for
    I'm seventy-five years old."

CAPTAIN EZEKIEL FLOUNDER

Upon the ocean's dip and swell
    The sailing ship *Belinda Bell*,
With Captain Flounder, grim and tanned,

In unconditional command,
Sailed every sea through calm and gale
    And never lost a single sail,
Because, whene'er a blow arose,
    The Captain knew it by his nose.

He claimed that he could smell a storm
    Of any pattern, size, or form.
And, truth to tell, he never failed,
    Until one day he calmly sailed
With every foot of canvas free
    Across the Caribbean Sea,
And then he got it in the neck—
    It happened on the forward deck.

The gaunt, bewhiskered Captain Zeke
    Took out a rag and blew his beak,
And, through his nostrils, old and thin,
    He blew a blast and then drew in
And nautically sniffed the breeze
    That rolled across the tranquil seas
And shouted to his meager crew,
    "I smell the weather; yes, I do."

"I see no sign of tempest rife,"
    Remarked the Captain's stocky wife.
She scanned the broad horizon's brim
    And saw no cloudlets, dark and grim.
"You're always smelling storms," she said.
    "You're rattled if the sky is red,
And when the northern lights come out
    You prophesy a waterspout."

The Captain gave a fearful snort
    And shot his orders, crisp and short,
"Let down them yards and furl the sails;
    We're headin' into Nor'east gales."
The crew obeyed without a flaw.
    They knew the skipper's word was law,
And soon the little sailing craft
    Was fit for weather, fore and aft.

"You're crazy like a lunatic,"
    Remarked his wife. "You make me sick.
There never was a fairer day,
    Since God Almighty made the bay.
There ain't the sign of airy squall

33

With power to overturn a yawl.
You'd better take a sip of tea
    And leave this sailin' job to me."

The skipper blew his nose once more
    And shouted in a muffled roar:
"You go below and shut your trap.
    I wasn't born to be a sap.
I'll prove to you my trusty nose
    Reports before the tempest blows,
And now you duffers better click
    And sink that anchor mighty quick."

The skipper's roly-poly wife,
    With tongue as sharp as any knife,
Unloosed a brand of language then
    That really cowed those stalwart men.
For once the skipper, bold and brave,
    Gave way before this verbal wave.
For once the sailors stood aghast,
    Bewildered by the blatant blast.

Across the deck with measured tread
    The woman firmly strode, and said:
"The Captain of this goddam ship
    Has got a nose that has the pip.
He thinks he smells a coming storm
    On days like this one, fair and warm.
His nose, afflicted with the plague,
    Just couldn't smell a rotten egg."

The ancient Captain shook his head.
    "Tobacco will decide," he said.
He held the plug beneath his nose
    And from that plug the odors rose.
He alternately whiffed and sniffed,
    And said, "I guess I'm all adrift.
I think you're right. I've lost my smell.
    I've got hay fever, sure as—anything!"

CAREFUL!

A glamour girl of modern style, alluring and alert,
With tact intrigued the stronger sex precisely where it hurt.
She ankled through the latest swing upon the stage and screen,
In plus abbreviated garb of evanescent sheen.

34

This winsome lass pursued her way unchallenged and serene,
But cruel fate can terminate a servant or a queen.
The glamour girl, accordingly, was severed from her kin.
She knocked upon Saint Peter's gate. Saint Peter let her in.

Credentials were requested, even those of queens and kings.
"I'll take a chance," Saint Peter beamed. Said she, "I'll take some wings."
"They're over there," Saint Peter gushed. "Pick out your size, my love."
She fumbled round and found a pair that fitted like a glove.

Saint Peter spoke: "My rules are strict and charm amounts to naught.
You'll lose those wings at once, if you possess one evil thought."
She coyly curtsied, whirled away. She heard a stifled cough,
And glanced around in time to see Saint Peter's wings fall off.

CAUTION

The ponderous Pacific is an awe-inspiring sight,
Gigantic in the daytime and repugnant in the night.
To ponder on its awful depth and vast amount of brine
Produces pain within my brain and shivers in my spine.

The Atlantic, by comparison, is just a limpid pool;
The Gulf Stream tones its temperature as if by magic rule.
Let those who brave Pacific waves with frigid mermaids sleep.
I'll travel the Atlantic which is not so cold and deep.

THE CHAMPION

Dick Shaw always sported his fisherman's hat
In his neat little camp by the vale.
He knew every instant just where he was at,
When he went on a pickerel trail,
For fishing the ponds and streams round about
Was always his fondest delight,
And he knew just the instant the bass and the trout
Were surely most likely to bite.

Now Dick had a way that was clearly his own
For pulling the biggest ones in,
But he always insisted on fishing alone,
Which caused all his neighbors chagrin.
He'd fish in the shallows and pull in a beaut

And then, from deep water, his mate.
But he weighed every one so there'd be no dispute,
When his story he chanced to relate.

Now Dick bright and early had started one morn
For the fishing grounds all sole alone.
It happened that day that a baby was born
In the camp next adjoining his own.
The parents, of course, were delighted and proud,
As his features they proudly surveyed.
But having no scales they protested aloud:
'Twas a shame he couldn't be weighed.

But then it occurred to the sweet little wife
That Dick had a weighing device.
So dad made the speediest trip of his life
And arrived at Dick's camp in a trice.
He found Dick away, but his scales were right there,
So returning by leaps and by bounds,
He balanced those scales with the greatest of care,
And the baby weighed twenty-five pounds.

CHAUFFEUR

Out of work, he accosted a lassie,
Who was winsome and certainly classy.
    With a nod of his head,
    He gallantly said,
"I can't help admiring your chassis."

Said she, "You're an ace at admiring;
You may note that my sparkplugs are firing;
    All my cylinders purr,
    But I have a chauffeur
With no notion at all of retiring."

CHICKEN POSSIBILITIES

When the snow is on the meadow, fifteen inches deep or more,
And the wind is whistling madly just outside the cottage door,
That's the time you feel like resting and your irksome labors shirk,
And you wish to goodness gracious that you needn't go to work.

By the time you get the snowdrifts shoveled out so you may pass,
Comes a sleetstorm which continues till the roads resemble glass,
And your flivver slides and slithers till you fear you'll over go;
It's a toss-up which is better—glassy ice or drifted snow.

But no matter what encounters, you must hustle to your job,
And you can't be late a minute, or you'll mingle with the mob
That consists of down-and-outers who are traveling the streets,
Each with feelings dire and mournful and quite vague concerning "eats."

This is not a pretty picture I have penned for you to read.
It may be exaggerated but it's partly true indeed.
Many men are sadly working where they're feeling far from gay,
When they might be watching leghorns as they golden nuggets lay.

Just imagine how enchanting such a job would feel to you.
And 'twould make no mortal difference if the howling blizzards blew.
You'd just watch the balanced rations vanish down a chicken's beak
And deliver in your flivver eggs and broilers twice a week.

And you'd pick your time for going, like the middle of the day,
No more half-past-seven journeys in the morning dark and gray.
You would be as independent as a yacht upon the swell,
While your steady-working pullets manufactured eggs to sell.

So get busy with the chickens and be free to come and go,
When the sun is in the zenith, melting down the drifted snow.
With good care and balanced rations, many eggs will fast appear;
With their combs as red as roses, you could have a banner year.

CHILD

I think no one will ever see
A lovely poem or a tree
Supremely charming as a child,
A little, winsome wonder-child.

A child who, blest with tender grace,
Upturns a thoughtful, trusting face,
Inquiring what the answer be
To each perplexing mystery.

A little child in Nature's plan
Brings boundless pride and joy to man.
The toddling steps of tiny feet
Leave footprints on Love's Memory Street.

A worthy poem lives on and on.
A lovely tree in time is gone,
Save one, of which the child must be
The savior. 'Tis the Family Tree.

CHILDREN

(Written on his 90th birthday, May 18, 1962)

I've lived and loved for ninety years,
And now, as elderness appears,
My darling wife at seventy-nine
Declares that she is feeling fine.
We've had our share of righteous joys:
Four lovely girls, five wondrous boys.
We'll step aside and let them shine
In every way, in every line.

We know they're smart and up-to-date.
We hope they'll steer our ship of state
Across the shoals, without a flaw,
Exactly like their dad and maw.
We hope they'll cling to actions fine
And never step across the line.
And this is sure, without a doubt:
'Twould be no fun to bail them out.

CHRISTMAS

Hark! I hear a tiny tinkling
Coming down the chimney flue;
Now watch out, for in a twinkling
Santa Claus may come in view.

He's the dearest, sweetest Santa,
And he loves good girls and boys.
With his reindeer on the canter,
He'll distribute loads of toys.

How we look and watch and listen,
When we know he's in our town;
And our eyes will surely glisten,
When he brings our presents down.

For he always knows precisely
What we've wished for all the year,
And then wraps them up so nicely;
Santa surely is a dear.

THE CHRISTMAS TREE

Across the landscape, broad and vast,
The Christmastime has come at last.
Where Christians emphasize the right,
The Christmas tree will spread its light.

The Christmas tree has come to stay;
Don't try to throw its charm away.
That yearly symbol is the sign
That all is right for yours and mine.

We elders try to keep alight
The legend of the Christmas night.
And little children love to see
The brilliant lighted Christmas tree.

The Christian spirit in the trees
Is wafted on the Christmas breeze.
Without the trees the Christmas cheer
Will merely add another year.

CHRISTMAS TREE DECISION

"Oh, yes—we have some Christmas trees;
These here we're proudly showing.
We also have a nursery,
Where Christmas trees are growing.
Here, take this saw and wander 'round
Among the rustic spruces.
Perhaps you'll find a lovely tree
Designed for Yuletide uses."

"We'll look these over first, I guess.
Now, here's one really nifty,
But now let's see the others, ere
We spend a dollar-fifty."
They feverishly squint and gaze

With every tree rejected.
Within an hour they're back and take
The one they first inspected.

CHRISTMASTIME

Christmastime has come again; we all must thankful be.
The Christian people of the earth prepare the Christmas tree,
And from its boughs will hang the gifts denoting friendships true,
A custom that's been carried down the long, long ages through.

It's not the value of a gift in monetary scale
That counts at all; the spirit of the giver must prevail.
A thousand-dollar gift is but a hollow, meanless thing,
Unless it comes from friend sincere and heartfelt greetings bring.

A smile, just nothing but a smile, will often bring more cheer
Than loads of gifts without the touch of friendship lingering near.
A kindly word from out the heart to one whose life is sad
Will bring more joy than all the wealth the Pharaohs ever had.

Christmastime has come again; our chance is now at hand
To broadcast joy and happiness to friends throughout the land.
But we must all remember that the gifts most worth the while
Are those that come well wrapped in love and given with a smile.

COLORADO RIVER

Between my banks, with righteous roar
    From Colorado's valleys,
Through Arizona's canyon core
    I make my plunging sallies.
To giant trees along my fringe
    My moisture is a blessing,
And flowering plants of radiant tinge
    Respond to my caressing.

Time was when Indians roamed abroad
    Astride their buckskin saddles.
They camped upon my verdant sward.
    My face has felt their paddles.
I've met old winter's frigid blast
    And basked in summer's weather.
I've watched the cloudlets drifting past,
    As we rolled on together.

40

For centuries no sacrifice
    Deprived me of devotion.
My head reposed in paradise;
    My feet were in the ocean.
I long enjoyed the prominence
    That mighty rivers cherish;
But now, deprived of all defense,
    I see my prestige perish.

The engineers have placed a dam
    Across my elevation,
A monstrous, cruel diaphragm
    That dulls my circulation.
They pipe my life-blood to the plains
    For irrigation uses.
My shriveling arteries and veins
    Collapse at these abuses.

I labored long to make my bed,
    Where I might lie and slumber.
My body, now, is being bled
    By farmers without number.
I'm bound and held by concrete bands
    At greedy man's dictation.
They've sent me over barren lands
    To succor vegetation.

I feel averse to giving blood
    In such unstinted measure.
I'm forced to manufacture mud
    Which adds to my displeasure.
I pray to God that melting snow
    May bolster my ambition,
And someday I will overflow
    And send them to perdition.

COMMON SENSE

As you speed along life's pathways,
Some are smooth and some are rough.
As you meet the various people,
Some are mild and some are gruff.
But you can't expect to mingle
With this crowd without expense;
So it's best to be prepared
With a lot of common cents.

41

COMPANIONS

Two farmer boys of tender age lived on adjoining farms.
Two hundred acres each contained. Each boasted equal charms.
Both farms were fertile, well laid out, productive, all walled in.
They'd made their owners well-to-do, Steve Hall and Billy Winn.
But Steve and Bill were getting old. They had not long to stay.
So little Steve and little Bill soon had the bills to pay.
And when the old folks went across the Jordan, to the Throne,
Both little Steve and little Bill had farms their very own.
Now little Steve and little Bill were made of different stuff.
While Steve was always satisfied, Bill never had enough.
Bill started out to make things hum. He cut the saplings down;
His pastures were his joy and pride, the slickest in the town.
But Stephen let the saplings grow. He didn't care at all.
He wasn't going to wrench his back to hear a sapling fall.
And so they farmed it side by side. Bill kept a lot of cows,
And turkeys, guinea hens and ducks, and goats and sheep and sows,
While Stephen got along quite well by trading with the guys,
Who thought they surely knew it all, until he put them wise.
Now Bill had scrimped for many years, and worked and toiled and slaved,
Until one day he reckoned up! Ten thousand plunks he'd saved.
And then and there he made a vow. "I'm going to take a rest.
I'll travel north and south, and then I'll travel east and west."
He called upon his neighbor, Steve. "I'm going to quit," he said.
"I've worked like fury all my life, and now, before I'm dead,
I'm going to visit all the spots from Concord to Hong Kong.
If you had worked as hard as I, you too might come along."
Next morning Steve gets out of bed and into town he trots;
He goes to see a lumberman, who buys up timber lots.
"I've got some timber on my farm. It's mostly pine and ash.
I plan to take a little trip, and need a bunch of cash."
Next day the lumberman came out and through the timber strayed.
And thirty thousand dollars was the figure that he paid.
So Stephen called on neighbor Bill, and said, while shaking hands,
"I think I'll ramble with you on your trip to foreign lands."
The moral of this little rhyme can easily be found.
It lies between the crooked lines the plow makes on the ground.
It also lies above the roots of saplings left to grow.
So take your pick and then decide which way your son shall go.

THE CONGRESSMAN

The congressman to hold his own
Would seem to be in duty bound
To keep one ear upon the phone
And park the other on the ground.

Constituents are hardy crews
From town or city, farm or ranch;
They send their congressman their views,
A veritable avalanche.

The congressman has many friends;
His secret is to hold them fast,
And reelection all depends
Upon the way their votes are cast.

His conscience plays a minor role
As guidance in affairs of state.
He reckons it his treasured goal
To keep his name upon the slate.

The congressman has many qualms,
When called upon to daily serve
The urbanites and folks on farms,
Who often have unbounded nerve.

They seem to think he holds the key
To every lock that guards a prize,
And if he sponsors something free,
They sing his praises to the skies.

The congressman who's worth his salt
Pays strict attention to decrees.
When legislation is at fault,
He's seldom with the absentees.

But many can't be counted in
By scratching with a fine-tooth comb.
They're guilty of the awful sin
Of building fences back at home.

The congressman who draws his pay
For helping pass a noxious tax,
And spends his moments far away
Deserves to feel the sharpened axe.

Often the congressman will wince,
When he has added up his score.
He'd better take some timely hints,
If he expects to serve some more.

The congressman who's up to date
Will join his colleagues who are true;
They're showing certain signs of late,
With pussyfooting they are through.

They'd better drop the yes-man stuff
And use some plain old common sense.
We hope chicanery and bluff
Will see their finish shortly hence.

COUÉ CURE

I was born in Massachusetts, and I'm glad with all my heart.
I've had my share of pleasures, and of toil I've done my part.
I used to have the best of health; my friends were staunch and true.
My farm is on the finest hill beneath the heavens blue.
I've had so many earthly joys I cannot count them all.
In spring I've sown and then I've reaped the harvest in the fall.
But now I'm growing old and gray. My footsteps sadly lag.
My back is bent, and at my knees there is a sickly sag.

When I was young I took a wife, the sweetest in the land.
We gaily started on our wedding journey hand in hand.
Our wedding trip was one grand spree; we traveled far away.
'Twas long before we journeyed back to Massachusetts Bay.
And when at last we reached our home at dear old Maple Hill
Our cup of joy was flowing o'er. Our love was stronger still.
But now the ravages of time have crushed my youthful frame.
My shaking hand can scarcely hold a pen to write my name.

Then after we were married soon the children came along.
Oh! what a joy it was in teaching them the right from wrong.
And through the winter evenings what a jolly time we passed,
All safe and warm, while out-of-doors the snow was falling fast.
And, oh! what jolly times we used to have on summer days,
While mingling with the kiddies in a thousand different ways.
But now my joints are bulging out. My fingers frail and numb
No longer grasp the steering wheel. I'm surely on the bum.

44

I wrote these lines some time ago; since then there's been a change.
I am now as husky as a grizzly bear upon the range.
No more my muscles fail to guide my former trembling hands.
My fingers on the steering wheel are firm as iron bands.
Each day new joy in life I find. My sleep is sound and sweet.
I'm growing younger every day, and lighter on my feet.
I'm confident my system will for many years endure.
And all because I heard about the famous Coué cure.

COUNTRY JOYS

Though city life has many thrills,
The countryside possesses charm;
So out among the verdant hills
I spent a week upon a farm.
The food was good. The country folk
Did all they could for my desire,
And through the evening many a joke
Was cracked before the open fire.

My stay was pleasant, till at last
The gathering clouds predicted rain.
Unless the farmer labored fast,
He'd have to dry his hay again.
I found a fork that looked all right
And to the field made utmost haste.
I figured by the lightning light
We'd have but little time to waste.

I speared a tempting bunch of hay.
The fork went through and speared my shin,
And I can show a scar today
Embedded deeply in my skin.
I tried again and struck a rock,
The force of which dislodged my hat.
The fork, rebounding from the shock,
Destroyed my glasses, just like that.

The wagon moved along its way
And left my hay pile lying there.
I found another pile of hay
And vowed to use the utmost care.

45

I pitched it to its proper place
And felt a spray of bugs and seeds
That crashed upon my upturned face.
The farmer calmly drawled, "Them's weeds."

I chased that wagon 'round the lot
With crickets running down my spine,
My throbbing temples burning hot,
My whole anatomy in brine.
I labored till my bindings burst.
My throat had symptoms of catarrh.
They gave me then to quench my thirst
Molasses mixed with vinegar.

At last the load was in the barn.
I parted from my trusty fork;
So now to finish up this yarn
A little secret I'll uncork.
When broad Gibraltar once again
In molten form glides far astray,
Upon that date, but not till then,
I'll pitch another load of hay.

COUSINS

When the cousins get together for a round-up of ideas,
You can hear no notes of anguish; you can see no dripping tears.
Every cousin has a mission, which she wants to spread afar,
And her intuition steers her to the empty cookie jar.

Then she tells her sister cousins how those cookies fill the bill
And the recipe is simple if they use a little skill;
And for other dainty dishes her advice is sharp and keen,
For she really knows the answer, if you know just what I mean.

All the cousins rate perfection in the modern cooking art;
In concocting brand-new mixtures they're always mighty smart.
They will mix a mess of cereals and shorten that with oil,
Then season it with sassafras and put it on to boil.

Now when it's done they dump it out and roll it flat and thin,
Then cut it into curlicues and smother them with gin.
A dash of four-leaf clover juice will add a pleasant smell
And toasted crisp and brown will make them delicate as anything.

These cousins hang together like a bunch of Concord grapes,
Though they differ from each other as to heights and widths and shapes,
But in cooking none acknowledge they will take the backward seats,
When it comes to seeking sponsors for delectable recipes.

So get ready with your answers; send a rule for frying ice,
And a quiet tip on juveniles would be extremely nice.
Can you cousins give the answer to the world's most pressing quiz?
When you drink a mug of lager, what becomes of all the fizz?

DEACON JONES AT BAT

Old Deacon Jones's youngest son
With joy o'erflowed at each home run
    His teammates batted out,
And what seemed more delightful still
When he, himself, with batting skill
    Produced a circuit clout.

Old Deacon Jones went out one day
To watch his son and cronies play
    And see the curves they threw.
At once his frame began to itch
To grasp a bat and solve the pitch
    And take a swing or two.

He waddled over to the plate
(A sad reminder of his gait
    Before he'd grown so fat),
"I used to hit 'em on the nose.
I'd like to swing a coupla blows,"
    He mumbled, just like that.

Then answered Stephen Haseltine,
A batter on the rival nine,
    "You, sir, may take my place."
"I'm much obliged," the Deacon said.
He took the bat while joy o'erspread
    The wrinkles on his face.

The memories of bygone years,
The loud applause, the welcome cheers
    His reveries awoke.
He heard a most derisive shout;
"Just watch Delaney strike you out."
    'Twas Junior Jones who spoke.

47

The pitcher didn't deign to wait,
But drilled a curve across the plate.
    Strike one. How well he knew.
The nervous twirler whirled again,
Straight down the alley lane, and then
    The old refrain: strike two.

Upon his hands the Deacon spat.
He firmed his grip upon the bat
    And grimly waited there,
And then the pitcher sent one through;
A whack! A crack! and toward the blue
    The pellet split the air.

Above the sprawling railroad shops,
Above the towering chimney tops
    The ball began its flight;
And toward the gorgeous setting sun,
As though its course had just begun,
    It soared to dizzy height.

The Deacon's gaze o'ertook the ball,
Its lightning rise, its fading fall
    Toward some far distant place.
Astonishment, then keen delight,
As ball continued on its flight,
    Pride decked the Deacon's face.

A cheer arose upon the air,
As Deacon Jones stood beaming there,
    A halo round his head.
He reeled. He fell, as in a faint,
And folded up without a plaint.
    Could Deacon Jones be dead?

But, no. He stirred, and Deacon Jones
Regained his feet 'mid grunts and groans,
    And in a trembling drawl
Observed, "On bats I'm rather keen,
And that's the liveliest bat I've seen.
    We'll need another ball."

DEACON VAN NESS

Old Deacon Van Ness wasn't timid or slow.
He never sidestepped any promise of "dough."
He'd lend a man currency any old day.
He knew a good mortgage was always O.K.
One time he loaned money to Benjamin West,
Took a mortgage on everything Benny possessed.
But Benny, unable to meet his demands,
Left Deacon Van Ness with a farm on his hands.

Now Deacon Van Ness spread no cries of alarm.
He sold out his home and moved out to the farm.
But farming he found was a different chore
From anything he had attempted before.
His pigs were all thin with their bones sticking through,
And his horses were suitable only for glue.
With cows drying up and his hens on the fritz,
His wifey insisted on calling it quits.

Along came a farmer who'd been a success.
He stopped to interrogate Deacon Van Ness.
"And how are things coming?" he cheerfully spoke.
The Deacon replied, "In a week I'll be broke."
He told of his troubles in desperate tones.
"My critters are starving; they're nothing but bones.
They go for that grain like you'd think they would bust,
Then spit it all out in apparent disgust."

"What grain are you using?" the farmer broke in.
"I get it from Southerlund, Cronin, and Quinn.
I think it is sawdust, of very poor grade."
"It's well," said the farmer, "I came to your aid.
Your SCQ fodder's not worth a good damn.
Change to QED grain and get out of your jam.
Don't tarry a second but hasten to town
And bring back a load. It has gained world renown."

Old Deacon Van Ness bounded into his truck
And made a beeline for the fountain of luck.
A QED member escorted him in.
Old Deacon Van Ness looked around with a grin.
"I hear that your grain ain't all sawdust and trash,"
He said as he fondled a bundle of cash.
"Just fill up that truck from the best of your stock,
And I'll test it out well on my critters and flock."

49

That grain had more oomph than the Deacon had guessed.
In a week there were eggs overflowing each nest.
The milk spouted out with no squeezing from him,
And his porkers no longer were bony and slim.
His team ran away and his bull had the gall
To toss the old Deacon right over the wall;
And things got so hot it was perfectly plain
He'd have to cut down on that wonderful grain.

The moral, of course, isn't hard to disclose.
If beset by uncertainties, troubles, and woes,
Don't listen to people abounding in lies,
And take advice only from those who are wise.

THE DEER SEASON

The time will come, just after dawn,
O'er windswept glade or wooded glen,
The right to slay the buck and fawn
Has been decreed to maids and men.
Protection laws on deer are nil.
The nimble creatures now must flee.
No more they'll graze the grassy hill
With furtive glance at you and me.

A few will fall, an easy prey;
The others, sensing danger then,
Will whisk their tails and haste away
To hide within the ferny fen—
Among the shadows, dark and dense—
Where hunters seldom penetrate.
They seem to have a seventh sense
Which saves them from a cruel fate.

The hunter now must make his way
Through tangled brush and swampy glade.
He knows his ever-watchful prey
Is hiding in that ambuscade;
And then a fern is slightly stirred—
The gun to shoulder—deadly aim—
And now a sharp report is heard,
A rush to claim the fallen game.

50

Perhaps a breeze has moved the fern—
Perhaps a deer, perhaps a hare;
Perhaps the marksman will discern
A fellow hunter, dying there.
The deed is done, no help in sight;
Remorse beclouds a human brain.
The hunter, overcome by fright—
Bewildered, sinks beneath the strain.

It isn't safe to draw a bead,
Because a twig is swayed or bent.
Let hunters take the utmost heed
And needless accidents prevent.
Let those who licenses acquire
Resolve to take the greatest care
To ascertain, before they fire,
Exactly what's in hiding there.

DEPRESSION—1933

It isn't hard to understand
    How this Depression came about.
There's ample proof on every hand;
    Of that there's not the slightest doubt.
The banks with coin are overstocked;
    Yet all the bankers are afraid.
They keep their safe-deposits locked
    Against expansion in the trade.

You cannot blame them much, at that,
    For man is timorous today.
He tours the town without a hat,
    Because it is the cheapest way.
He grimly wears his threadbare suits
    And meets his friends without a flinch.
He daily shines his antique boots.
    He isn't spending; that's a cinch.

Time was when men in every walk
    Had courage to invest their cash,
But now they spend their time in talk
    About the crazy Wall Street crash.

Their old-time zip is dead and gone.
    Depression-minded tells the tale—
They simply sit and stretch and yawn,
    While daring not to spend their kale.

It's just the same with women, too;
    Each dollar spent invokes a sigh.
Their purchases are precious few,
    And bare necessities they buy.
They shorten up their ancient skirts,
    Or let them down and mend the holes.
They save and save until it hurts,
    But on deposit keep their rolls.

Time was when womenfolk were keen
    To keep their prestige on parade.
They'd circulate the filthy green
    And help to turn the wheels of trade.
They'd break a twenty, ten, or five
    With callous coolness heretofore,
But now like bees around a hive
    They patronize the ten-cent store.

The tailors now are doused in gloom.
    The hatter's hats are on the shelf.
The hairpin merchants sense their doom.
    The shoe stores salt away no pelf.
And many a man who feels inclined
    To treat his stomach to a feast
Will find a post to hide behind
    And gobble down a cake of yeast.

DESERVING FARMER

The farmer totes a heavy load; adversity is his. He has no classy, secret code to aid him in his "biz." He toils from early morn till night and takes his pay in praise, for everyone shows pure delight in crops the farmers raise.

The farmer claims he's on the verge of failure, dark and dim. Without relief the funeral dirge will soon be sung for him. We must not let him peter out; no one could take his place. The farms alone, without a doubt, must feed the human race.

The farmer's life is chiefly spent in warfare, gruff and grim. Potato bugs and such are sent to crush and conquer him. The dreaded blight and fungus fuzz upon his vines alight, and all day long the sprayer buzz proclaims a losing fight.

The cutworms chew his pumpkin shoots and never come in view. The grubs devour his cabbage roots and beets and parsnips too. The crows and blackbirds and the jays pull up his corn and beans. By harvest time he's drenched in praise with nothing in his jeans.

The farmer's job is planting seeds; he gambles not nor bets. He tussles with the devilish weeds and earns whate'er he gets. Production is his cherished goal. He shows unbridled zeal. He doesn't crave the bulging roll, but wants an equal deal.

His very life depends on us and he's a decent guy; so let's not make a fearful fuss if cauliflowers are high. Let's help the farmer with his load a-toiling up the hill, and, when we meet him on the road, a little reverence spill.

DEVOTION

That night a vivid picture met my eyes,
    As from the path I noticed in surprise
Old Zeke Palenta poring o'er a book,
    That ugly ancient reprobate and crook.

By lighted lamp that spread depressing gloom,
    He scanned those pages in that squalid room,
Where flies foregathered from the outside chill
    By crevice, crack, and crumbling windowsill.

The open doorway beckoned my advance,
    As there I paused astounded, as a glance
Depicted, by the lamp's insipid rays,
    The Holy Bible occupied his gaze.

My breathing must have made the slightest sound.
    Old Zeke with palsied motion looked around.
He closed the Holy Book with trembling hands
    And hissed, "I found nine hundred goddam 'ands.'"

DISAPPOINTMENT

We've got a daughter, Mary Ann,
Which wan't accordin' to our plan.
I know a boy would save us dough;
He'd help to milk and weed and hoe.
But good intentions ain't so hot,
For just a girl is what we got,
An' what makes me so gorram mad,
At times I think her maw is glad!

A girl, o' course needs lots o' cloes
An' lotions for her cheeks an' toes.
A boy don't need no folderols;
He's right to home in overalls.
A boy is diff'rent from a gal.
He makes his paw a dandy pal.
Although a girl is quite a drain,
I s'pose I orter not complain.

But still there's just a chance I'm wrong.
I'm positive we'll get along.
I've got machines of every kind
To sow and weed and reap and grind.
'Twould take a boy some little time
To grow enough for spreadin' lime
An' fixin' harrows, plows an' rakes,
An' testin' tractor bands and brakes.

O' course a girl would be no use
When reaper parts was gettin' loose.
I can't help thinkin' what a joy
It woulda been to had a boy;
But, I dunno, she's purty cute
A-cooin' in that fluffy suit.
Her cheeks are round an' fair an' fat.
I guess the Lord knows what He's at.

DREAMER

Mr. Hiram Moses Mello
Was a young, progressive fellow.
A town meeting he attended brought discomfort to his soul,

For the way they squandered money
Didn't qualify as funny,
As the necessary taxes left him deeply in the hole.

As he grew in mind and stature,
He became a train dispatcher,
A responsible position that a steppingstone became.
Later on he was promoted
To a calling, sugar-coated,
But he never ceased to marvel at the politician's game.

Mr. Mello was delighted
When associates invited
Him to run for minor office as a step to greater heights.
But his slogan, "Win with Moses,"
Failed to sprout election roses.
He got trimmed and hastened homeward and extinguished all the lights.

But a man with his ambition,
Who believed he had a mission
To enlighten all the people who were taxed to pay the bills,
Never yielded to the rabble,
But enlisted in the scrabble
For the office of assessor, and was buried to the gills.

But his dander was arising
And his courage most surprising.
Next election found him running for the sheriff's juicy berth.
When the precious votes were counted,
His opponent's tally mounted,
Till he seemed to own the county and the nation and the earth.

For a certain time thereafter,
When he met a greedy grafter,
He would "high-hat" the deceiver who had robbed the public purse.
But his righteous indignation
Changed to major exultation,
When he knew a grafting demon was reposing in the hearse.

Mr. Mello took his trimmings
At the polls with sad misgivings.
In his business he was aces and had never known defeat.
Suddenly he had a vision
Which produced a quick decision;
So he made a sudden exit and went strutting down the street.

As Election Day was nearing,
People noticed him appearing
In most unexpected places at most unexpected times.
He glad-handed politicians,
Stating he had no ambitions
As to politics and hinted that he longed for southern climes.

Still he lingered, and his cronies
Grimly watched him play the ponies,
And he lost their admiration when he sought the gambling hall.
Word went round that Moses Mello
Was a regulation fellow,
And his enemies admitted he had something on the ball.

He threw parties for the muckers
Who had called the voters suckers,
And they promptly recommended Mr. Mello as their choice.
So he paid for all the banners
And a carload of "Havanas,"
And addressed so many rallies that he nearly lost his voice.

When the ballot battle ended,
Mr. Mello had expended
Several barrels of mazuma, but he didn't get the gate,
For his underworld defenders,
Of all well-established genders,
Had elected him to mayor by the largest vote to date.

Then the graft began to tumble
With a rather muffled rumble
Straight into His Honor's pockets where it burned no conscience holes.
After several years' collections,
He had failed to make connections
With the gang which made him mayor, and was hauled across the coals.

But he showed no signs of yielding,
And instead he started wielding
The big stick of self-importance and responded, "Let them hoot."
And he gave his ultimatum,
That he'd sure annihilate 'em,
If they didn't cease their howling for a portion of the loot.

Then he called a public meeting
And addressed them with this greeting,
"Here's the graft that I've collected, every dollar, every sou.
I have kept a strict accounting
And the figures still are mounting,
But I thought the time propitious for returning it to you."

There were shouts of indignation
From the grafting delegation,
And he bellowed in defiance, "I'm the shepherd for the sheep."
        Then he felt somebody shake him,
        And, in order to awake him,
Wifey said, "Roll over, dearest. You are talking in your sleep."

DOWN BY THE VALE

It was down by the vale where sweet breezes were gliding,
Where the murmuring stream rippled through the tall grass.
It was there where the jaybirds and hawks were abiding—
'Twas there where I happened to meet a sweet lass.
She was out after berries, those luscious red berries;
I might also say she was out after dark.
She was out at the elbows; her cheeks were like cherries.
And when she saw me she was out for a lark.

I gave her a bough from a tree that stood near me.
She gave me a sigh which she took from the pines,
Then dropped a remark which proceeded to cheer me—
We clinched on the spot where the lightning bug shines.
Oh, the sweet words she poured down my ear were inviting.
Bliss, joy, and contentment were filling my cup.
I was just getting ready to make things exciting—
When my wife sweetly whispered, "It's time to get up."

THE EAGLE

The eagle grasps the jutting crag with talonaceous grip.
Through storm and tempest, unafraid, he contemplates a trip
Far down below his friendly crag, within the valley strip.

An object meets his vision, which he holds with steady stare.
With folded wings he, arrow-like, descending, cleaves the air,
And well he knows his aim is true to meet the rabbit there.

EASTER

From the hillside and the valley, from the mountain and the plain
All the snow has vanished, and the welcome spring,
Bringing songbirds from the southern land, is with us once again;
'Tis a joyous time for every living thing.

All the little buds are bursting into life upon the trees,
And the flowers are awaking from their winter sleep,
While new joy and life are everywhere upon the balmy breeze;
For these blessings Easter Day we always keep.

THE ECLIPSE

The science of Man will impart to the World
What the recent eclipse to our people unfurled.
The strangest phenomena came into view,
As the rocky old Moon chased the Sun's rays askew.
The cows in the pasture strolled up to the bars,
Stood waiting for Tom with the milkpail and jars.
The hens and the chickens reluctantly fled,
Without any supper, right into the shed.

The rooster was puzzled and gazed 'round and 'round,
Then warned all the hens with a gurgling sound.
The cat and the dog went to sleep in the hay,
Apparently willing to call it a day.
The crickets came out, the grasshoppers went in,
And the tree-toads emerged for the night to begin.
The gay petting-parties disgustingly fared.
"Shortest session on record," they glumly declared.

The birds ceased their singing; the frogs came to life.
The gnats and mosquitoes prepared for the strife.
The screech owls saluted the foxes and coons,
And the whippoorwill whistled the shortest of tunes.
The sunflowers closed when the dewdrops appeared,
And the cabbageheads nodded as duskiness neared.
We all stood around or reclined on the grass
And squinted aloft through a piece of smoked glass.

But ninety-three seconds passed quickly away.
Before we all knew it, again it was day.
The hens reappeared with a mystified screech
And in no time at all laid another egg each.
The dog and the rest of the creatures as well
Came looking for breakfast as hungry as anything,
And the parkers in autos, chagrined at the light,
Rolled down to the city to come back at night.

The eclipse being over, we learned quite a lot,
And science will benefit, likely as not.
And now, my dear friends, here's the straightest of tips;
The whole blooming world is in total eclipse.
But do not despair, nor give up with a sigh.
There are rifts in the clouds. There is blue in the sky.
And before many moons all our troubles will cease,
And our lives will delight in prosperity's peace.

EDUCATION

Our thoughts and acts concerning facts about our glorious planet have
seen great change of scope and range since former people ran it. The
time has come when cloudy brain possessed by either John or Jane can
never great distinction gain, achievement carved in granite.

Skill comes to those who, on their toes, await the golden chances, and
study more to learn the score concerning world advances. The education
topic leads debate on what the nation needs, but controversy sows the
seeds of crazy circumstances.

Folks talk a lot on what is what regarding education. They rightly say
to live today requires a firm foundation. The surest way to lead the van
is storing knowledge while you can; so you won't be an also-ran in our
enlightened nation.

And seldom can the common man attain to high endeavor. A handicap
he has on tap which follows him forever. There's something lacking in
his bean. His love for knowledge isn't keen. He simply coasts and that
will mean he'll rise to prestige, never.

A man to be successful, he must start at the beginning and when
begun must score a run before the final inning. His brain must hold a
vast supply of intellect that's ranking high, or out he'll go upon a fly
and lose his chance of winning.

So, girls and boys, sidestep the joys and make your knowledge greater.
The time will come you'll pick a plum and praise your alma mater. With
education fill your net. You'll need it is the safest bet. Grab all the
schooling you can get, or you'll be sorry later.

EDWARD EARLE SOUTHWICK
(Four days old)

Well, Edward Earle,
You're not a girl,
But still I'll bet you'll have a curl
Upon your brow,
A perfect "wow"
When you're a little older.
But now I dare
To say your hair
Is rather straight and rather spare.
But later we
Shall ringlets see
Upon your grandpa's shoulder.

I know your Pa
And dear Mama
Are glad that it's a boy you are,
And so am I,
And that is why
I'm sending this epistle.
And when you grow,
I'll let you know,
Because your grandpa loves you so.
And this is true,
He'll make for you
A lovely willow whistle.

EIGHTY-SEVEN

Since I've arrived at eighty-seven
My next stop possibly is Heaven,
Or else that other place of note,
Where I shall need no overcoat.

But be it up or be it down,
When on my head they place a crown,
I know that I shall get a thrill
From memories of Maple Hill.

EXPECTATION

Ten thousand gather at the track
To watch the ponies win the "jack."
A thing, concerning far too few,
Is gazing on an empty pew.

The preacher in a troubled mood
Observes his ever-meager brood
And thoughts come coursing through his mind
How racing dogs attract mankind.

We mortals are a funny bunch
To place our bets upon a hunch.
We seem to think that when we die
The eulogy will let us by.

I feel quite sure no cruel fate
Will bar me from the Golden Gate.
I feel, although I'm steeped in sin,
On Mother's ticket I'll slip in.

FAIR PLAY

An Englishman and Irishman were arguing one day;
The bitterness suggested that the pistols come in play.
The Englishman demurred and said, "I'm twice the size of him.
What chance have I to hit a guy extremely tall and slim?"

The Irishman admitted that the targets weren't the same.
And said, "You big fat bloke, you're holding up the game.
Upon your front with chalk we'll draw a man the size of me,
To make two targets just the same. I hope you will agree.

"With trusty pistols we'll advance. The platform then we'll mount.
And any hits I chance to make outside the line won't count."

FAMILY GARDEN

Josephus Jones gave out advice
In phrases, pointed and precise,
    To friends, the other day.
He said if we'd be free from toil,

Just buy a little plot of soil
    Without undue delay,
And then with spade and fork and hoe
Prepare the land and mark each row
    With diligence and care,
Then plant the seeds, well fertilized,
And later on we'll be surprised
    At what is growing there.

He said one tiny pumpkin seed
Will raise more pumpkins than we'll need,
    And we can sell the rest.
He said one hill of lima beans
Will furnish us with ample means
    To fill our treasure chest.
He said no matter what we plant
Our feelings will be jubilant
    With thankfulness and praise.
Our cellars will be filled with chow
For uncles, cousins, kids, and frau
    Throughout the winter days.

I listened to Josephus Jones
Expound his views in earnest tones,
    But still I had to smirk.
He didn't mention worms and lice
And bugs and grubs and moles and mice
    That do their deadly work.
He didn't mention wind and drought
That make the tender plants die out.
    He didn't mention weeds.
But still with all these pesky ills
A well-groomed garden always fills
    A host of family needs.

THE FARM (1)

A few remarks I'd like to make about the patient farmer.
For quiet ways he takes the cake; no mortal could be calmer.
He plods along his chosen way in cool and cautious manner
And seldom future plans will lay without consulting Anna.
He counsels with his girls and boys in every undertaking,
And shares their trials and their joys through all his hours of waking.

The time has gone when heavy hand applied with vim and vigor
Can keep the children on the land when they've grown strong and bigger.
The farmer's job today is blest with modern stores of knowledge.
The son whose services are best has come from Farmer's College,
And daughter, too, has every chance to take a course at farming.
She'll not require the Charleston dance to make her chic and charming.
The farming game of yesterday no longer is in fashion.
No more can farms be made to pay by pummeling and passion.
It takes a cool, collected brain for farming operation
To raise the spuds and corn and grain and meat to feed the nation.
The modern methods now in use, the trusty truck and flivver,
The mystical electric juice to light and power deliver,
The graded roads of smooth cement throughout the country over
All help to make the kids content to reap the corn and clover.
Among the classy poultry flocks across the country scattered,
Rhode Island Reds and Plymouth Rocks have all the records shattered,
While Leghorns White and Buff and Brown from every section quarter
Have brought much profit and renown to farmer, son, and daughter.
The girl or boy who now decides to be a farm beginner
Can make his work his joy and pride and ramble home a winner;
While those who clamor for a job in office, store, or lobby
Will find they're members of the mob with five o'clock their hobby.
They'll spend their last remaining sou within the picture palace.
The girls will go with Ed or Lou, the boys with May or Alice,
While on the farm the radio will furnish education,
And girls and boys will save their dough for future speculation.
The farm. The farm. The glorious farm is tried and true and trusty.
It always has a home-like charm with praises loud and lusty.
So do not make the sad mistake of passing up its treasures,
With pumpkin pie and angel cake among its joys and pleasures.

THE FARM (2)

All around the earth we've wandered.
On life's problems we have pondered,
And much precious time we've squandered
Seeking scenes of greatest charm.
After being deftly guided
To the spots where we've abided,
We have finally decided
There's no haven like the farm.

There we meet each worthy neighbor
In the field of worthwhile labor.
We are there with gun and saber
Should the Nation call to arm.
We will give the foe no quarter
On the land or on the water.
We will pledge each son and daughter
To the service, from the farm.

But we're hoping and we're trusting
Warfare cruel and disgusting
Shall forever cease its lusting,
Shedding terror and alarm.
May the future tell the story
Of a wondrous peace-time glory,
Love conceived and mandatory
By example from the farm.

FARMER BRIGGS

Bartholomew Briggs had a farm in the vale. It chiefly consisted of swampland and swale. His farm was secured at a very low price, as all it would raise was mosquitoes and rice. Disgust wreathed the face of Bartholomew Briggs. He'd visioned a fortune from ponderous pigs, but water, alone, as a diet was punk. Bartholomew Briggs realized he was sunk.

A stranger drove over and turned off the switch. Said he, "Mr. Briggs, would you like to be rich? Just dam up the river and cover this mud; raise muskrats and money will come in a flood. Each muskrat possesses a sac filled with musk. You'll find that you'll labor from daylight to dusk to furnish the musk that is daily required by makers of perfume, so keenly desired."

Bartholomew Briggs took the stranger's advice. He dammed up the river in manner precise. The water flowed backwards and covered his land, to furnish the pond which the stranger had planned. As the water flowed in with a rush and a roar, his pigs floated upwards and swam to the shore. No traces of mud were apparent on each. They all seemed content as they basked on the beach.

After damming the river to furnish the flood that would cover his seventy-five acres of mud, he sent to Muskegon, the sensible place, to buy his supply of the musk-bearing race. The muskrats arrived by the truckload and van, and shortly thereafter his labors began. He dumped them all into their welcoming lair. 'Twas beyond all belief how they multiplied there.

The musk from those muskrats brought magic success. The pelts from those muskrats surpassed every guess. The meat from those muskrats was fed to the swine, which changed their appearance to favored design. Bartholomew Briggs is retired and at ease, absorbing the sunshine and Bermuda breeze. Parading the streets with his fur-adorned frau, he's known as the Musk Multi-Millionaire now.

FARMER JOE

"Will you direct me to the track
Where I can make a lot of jack
By simply putting up the dough
And watching while the ponies go?"
"Oh, sure," replied the dapper tout.
"You know the game, without a doubt,
But here's a quiet, little tip:
Put all your coin on NEVER SLIP."

"Just so, just so," said Farmer Joe,
"But where's the track? I'd like to know!"
"Of course!" replied the tout with glee.
"I'll show you if you'll follow me."
Across the city, down the pike,
They made an ankle-testing hike,
And later in the autumn air
They spotted Narragansett there.

Then Farmer Joe, a thoroughbred,
Together clicked his heels and said,
"I have two thousand berries here,
And they are bound to bring me cheer;
I play 'em straight across the book,
To breeze, to show, to place, to look,
And up and down and in and out."
"You crazy nut," remarked the tout.

But Farmer Joe was not dismayed
And through the wickers paid and paid.
On every entry in each race

He bet his cash at least to place.
His final twenty-dollar bill
Soon nestled in the bookie's till,
And straightway Farmer Joe rushed out
To watch the finish with the tout.

At last the races all were run,
And Farmer Joe commenced his fun.
He nimbly flitted to and fro
And cashed his slips for bales of dough,
And Farmer Joe was later seen
Departing in a limousine.
The bookies counted, when they quit,
Two thousand dollars counterfeit.

FARMER JOE'S LAMENT

My wife wan't any good no more.
She'd knocked her head agin' a door,
An' after that she wan't the same.
It also left her kinder lame.

The sink was full of grease an' grime.
She dropped the dishes all the time,
An' when she'd mop the kitchen floor
She'd lay right down an' snore an' snore.

She used to be right smart an' pert,
But ever since her head got hurt
I had to use her on the plow.
I'da liked to swap her for a cow.

One day a doctor happened by.
The wife come out, begun to cry.
"Well, what's the fuss?" the doctor said.
I told him that she'd struck her head.

The doctor in his soothin' tone
Remarked, "Perhaps she crushed a bone."
He fumbled 'round amongst her hair
An' said, "There's somethin' pressin' there."

He took her with him, there an' then,
An' said, "She'll soon be back again."
An' after waitin' quite a spell
He dropped a line that she was well.

Then back she come, all safe an' sound,
An', golly, how she knocks me 'round.
I hope she don't remember how
I used to use her on the plow.

FARMER LaPLANTE

Old Farmer LaPlante was prodigiously stout. The scales
Topped three hundred without any doubt. With bitter resentment
He'd grumble and groan, and never was happy at being alone.
As spry on his feet as a barrel of lime, he feared if he fell
He'd be there for all time. Though worries for some are
Depressing a lot, the greater *his* worries, the fatter he got.

A neighbor dropped in for a neighborly chat, and said, "There's
No sense in your being so fat; a marvelous cure for obesity's
Curse is available now and quite soft on the purse. No longer
Is fattiness out of control, with slender designing the ultimate
Goal." Then, after a pause and a moment's delay, with solemn
Regard he continued to say—

"Some feed-mixing people, exceedingly keen, can change a
Pig's fat into meat that is lean. Their VANISH is simply a diet,
They claim. Less fat and more lean is their ultimate aim.
Experiments show that their claims are all true. I haven't
A doubt it will work upon you. Sol Solomon's pigs are a sight to
Behold. He classifies VANISH as better than gold. He has
Doubled his sales with his profit a cinch, but not by the ton;
They are sold by the inch."

Then Farmer LaPlante, with a series of grunts, rolled over and
Said, "I'll try anything once, but restricting my diet is not
In my line; give me three squares a day and I'm fancy and fine.
But if VANISH can vanish the blubber from swine, it surely should
Vanish this blubber of mine. I don't care for magical
Streamlined effect, but just so my twenty-inch collars connect."

The neighbor then joyously scribbled some notes.
"I'll bring you the menu they use on their shoats.
You'll find it is filling and nourishing, too.
Your frame will resemble a slender bamboo."
Two months of that diet for Farmer LaPlante
Have given his torso a juvenile slant.

Two months of that diet was all that it took
To give him a dignified, muscular look.

67

He takes in the nightclubs and parties in stride,
Which he would have missed had he blown up and died.
He dances the tango and waltzes and jigs
By using the menu they fashioned for pigs.

FATHER'S NIGHT SONG

Here we are again. Brightly lighted hall.
See the jolly men. Welcome one and all.
Make yourselves at home. Keep your spirits light.
All the while just smile and smile, for this is Father's Night.

(Chorus)

Father's Night. Father's Night comes but once a year.
Throw the throttle open wide. Shift to highest gear—
Father's Night. Father's Night. Let us all be gay.
Shout and sing and courage bring—to the Leicester PTA.

Mothers always come. Fathers seldom do.
Oh! how things would hum—if they'd gather too.
Lovely would it be, meeting Fathers here.
That's the way for PTA to score a record year.

(Chorus)

Father's Night. Father's Night. We must loyal be.
Each should give a little time, heartily and free—
Father's Night. Father's Night. Let's all shout HOORAY!
We are here to bring good cheer to the Leicester PTA.

FEELIN' THAT'S APPEALIN'

When a man has traveled far and wandered here and there,
When he's lonely and his friends are scattered everywhere,
If he meets a bonny lass who has a winsome smile,
Why, he'd be foolish not to stop and tarry for a while.
What's the use to make excuse and say he doesn't care,
If he feels the strong appeal to stroke her golden hair?
What if she should friendly be the while he lingers there?
    'Twould surely be a feelin' that's appealin'.

Hoist the glasses steady now and sip the light champagne.
Everyone be ready now to fill them up again.
Just a little romance now a-trippin' down the lane,
　　'Twould surely be a feelin' that's appealin'.

When he finds the lassie listenin' to his travelin' tales,
While they're out a-strollin' through the verdant hills and dales,
Comin' home, it's nice to trip in step with such a lass,
While dreamin' of the wondrous things perhaps may come to pass.
Strollin' by the rollin' waves that wash the glitterin' sand,
Roamin' by the foamin' billows breakin' on the strand,
Flirtin' in a certain way and squeezin' of her hand,
　　'Twould surely be a feelin' that's appealin'.

When he finds that love has come and can't be turned aside,
And he asks the winsome lass if she will be his bride,
When she nestles closer yet and doesn't say a thing
It's easy then to slip her finger through the tiny ring.
Blessin' her, caressin' her, his feelings to convey,
Strokin' her and jokin' her to pass the time away,
Squeezin' her and teasin' her to quickly name the day,
　　'Twould surely be a feelin' that's appealin'.

FINAL INSTRUCTION

When I have cashed in all my checks,
I shall not care for creed or sex;
I shall not crave a velvet shave,
Nor silken undergarments;
I shall not kick where'er I lie
Beneath the sod or open sky;
I shall not cringe from gnawing twinge
Of microbes, worms, or varmints.

There's only one request I make,
Whether I play the harp, or bake;
Now here's the gist: I must insist
My funeral director
Shall heed this message from my soul—
"Be careful where you dig the hole.
Don't try to hide my bones beside
A gorram tax collector."

FINAL RACE

The jockey lay upon the straw, within one corner of the stall,
Where stood "The Monarch" restlessly awaiting soon the starter's call.
The jockey writhed in fearful pain. It seemed as tho his side would burst.
He felt the fever coming on; oh, for a drink to quench his thirst.
"The Monarch" stamped and pawed his straw, a racehorse bred of royal
strain,
With sinews stretched like bars of steel, with coat like silk from tail to
mane.
"The final race" was on that day. Five thousand pounds the purse to be.
The jockey moaned, "Oh, why this pain, when everything depends on
me?"
The sound of footsteps reached his ear. The grooms were coming. Now
the race.
The jockey tried to rise, but fell, with lines of torture on his face.
Two swarthy men came walking in; they saw the jockey on the hay.
"Wake up!" said one. "The race is on! 'The Monarch' sure must win
today!"
"I can't get up," the jockey said. 'The pain is fierce. I cannot stand."
"Brace up!" the other sternly spoke. "Brace up! Brace up! And show
your sand!"
"I can't. I can't," he said again. " 'Twill kill me if I ride today.
Go tell the boss I cannot ride. Go. Go at once. Do not delay."
"The boss will kill you. That he will. 'Tis only you can win this race.
Hark! here he comes. Get up! Get up! And save yourself from this
disgrace."
A portly man of massive frame came striding through the stable door.
He scarcely could believe his eyes to see the jockey on the floor.
"Get up! you lazy cur," he roared. "The race is on. D'you hear the bell?"
The jockey vainly tried to rise; he lurched one step, then backward fell.
"I cannot ride," the jockey said, with agony upon his face.
"Give him a shot! A double dose. 'Twill keep him up to win this race."
The deadly needle did its work. The jockey rose. The pain was gone.
"I'll do my best." His face was white. Upon the track the race was on.
"They're off! They're off!" "The Monarch" ran as never he had run before.
The quarter passed. The jockey swayed. Oh! can he last three-quarters
more?
The noble "Monarch" fairly flew. The half is passed. He leads the way.
The jockey whispered to himself, "I knew I should not ride today."
With mighty nerve he keeps his mount. Three-quarters of the race is
done.
"Oh! spare me twenty seconds more, and then I'll know that we have
won."
The horses turn into the stretch. "The Monarch" leads by half a length.

The jockey's grip upon the rein is gone. The pain has sapped his strength.
On! On! they come, across the tape. "The Monarch" wins five thousand
    pounds.
But, look! His head is high in air; the jockey lies upon the ground.
On come the rest. They cannot stop. Each horse must finish in his place.
The cruel hoofs. A mangled form. The jockey won "the final race"?

FISHERMAN

Once a fisherman lay dying on his hard and humble cot,
And the pastor sat beside him saying things that hit the spot,
So that all his futile terrors left the dying sinner's heart,
And he said, "The journey's lonely, but I'm ready now to start.
But there's just one little matter that is fretting me," he sighed.
"And perhaps I'd better tell it, ere I cross the Great Divide.
I have a string of stories that I've told from day to day,
Stories of the ones I've captured and the ones that got away.
And I fear that when I tell them they are apt to stretch a mile,
And I wonder when I'm wafted to the land that's free from guile,
If they'll let me tell my stories, if I try to tell them straight,
Or will angels lose their tempers, then, and chase me through the gate."
Then the pastor sat and pondered, for the question vexed him sore.
Never such a weird conundrum had been sprung on him before.
Yet the courage of conviction moved him soon to make reply,
And he wished to fill the fisher with fair visions of the sky.
"You can doubtless tell your stories," said the clergyman quite loud,
"And they'll stand a lot of stretching too, if Jonah's in the crowd."

FLESH AND BLOOD

Josephus Jones and Mrs. Jones
Bewailed the fact, in doleful tones,
    That they must childless stay.
Still, others had been reconciled
By the adoption of a child.
    This seemed the only way.

They gave the problem deepest thought,
Declaring that the child they sought
    Must have no evil stain.
And Providence, forever kind,
Enabled them in time to find
    A child of worthy strain.

71

They straightway summoned Doctor Bones
Who oft administered to Jones
    And likewise to his wife.
A consultation then ensued
With lofty sentiments imbued.
    Out came the grafting knife.

A tiny piece of flesh and skin
From mama's arm was grafted in
    On baby's tender heel.
A blood transfusion, oh, so wee,
From papa Jones's artery
    He wrought for baby's weal.

The baby thrived as babies should
And grew to charming maidenhood,
    And womanhood as well.
No finer type could words portray,
And papa Jones is proud to say,
    "Yes, flesh and blood will tell."

FLYING SAUCERS

My wife and I were strolling through a field of waving
Grass, when suddenly to westward there appeared a moving
Mass, which speedily approached us with a weirdly hissing
Sound. The moonlight marked its passage fifty feet above
The ground. We rushed beneath a giant tree whose limbs
Spread far and wide, and I am not ashamed to say we both
Were terrified. Then, trembling at the very thought, my
Wife made out to say, "We've seen a flying saucer and no
Man may say us nay."

The saucer vanished easterly, but ere we got our breath
It came a-roaring back again. We sensed a sudden death.
Its course was slightly lower now and nearer than before,
And as it passed our refuge we were deafened by the roar.
Its speed was so extremely swift our vision failed to click.
No telescope, however strong, could then have turned the trick.
As back and forth that saucer flew in ever smaller arcs,
We felt quite sure that we could smell the fumes from
Brimstone sparks.

Just then it took another twist and circled overhead.
It cut a loop and toward a radio station sped.
Its course was straightway for the tower. We saw a
Brilliant flash, and waited just an instant for the
Devastating crash, but luckily it soared aloft before it
Reached the tower, and vanished in the distance and was
Gone for half an hour. We didn't leave our precious tree;
That disc was full of tricks. To meet a flying saucer in
An open field was nix.

But half an hour is quite a while in anybody's book.
We stealthily advanced a bit and took a hurried look.
We reasoned that a half a mile to home we couldn't miss,
But scurried backward when we heard that same familiar hiss.
That flying demon made a swoop and barely missed us then.
It clipped some branches from our tree and whirled aloft again.
We huddled closely to that trunk. Our throbbing blood ran cold.
And that, my friends, unfolds the biggest lie I ever told.

THE FOREST (1)

The level, fertile plain,
    Of course, is needed,
For here the golden grain
    Is yearly seeded.
Mankind must till the soil
    To feed the Nation.
The product of such toil
    Is our salvation.

The treeless slope and hill
    Skirt verdant hollows,
Where many a rock-bound rill
    Earth's contour follows.
These sections we must keep
    For livestock raising,
Where horses, cattle, sheep
    May do their grazing.

But give me forest trees,
    Tall pines and larches,
And sermons preached by these
    'Neath sylvan arches.

God raised the trees, sublime,
  With Nature's leaven.
Give me tall trees that climb
  From Earth toward Heaven.

THE FOREST (2)

Deciduous trees, the maples, oaks, and ashes,
Discard their clothing over frozen field
And, unashamed, in lightning's brilliant flashes
Stand stark with all their nakedness revealed.

The evergreens, the lofty pines and spruces,
Have all the rules of etiquette obeyed
And consequently offer no excuses,
When joining in the forestry parade.

When springtime's warmth in quantity unstinted
Is wafted over mountainside and glen,
Those shameless trees with leaves divinely tinted
Appear in all their dignity again.

The forest calls a spring arboreal meeting,
Which every known variety attends.
The pines and spruces wave a cordial greeting,
Thus welcoming their newly tailored friends.

FROLICKING LASSIES

I travel afar over land and sea,
And the places I visit appeal to me,
But keeping forever my memory sweet
Are the frolicking lassies I chance to meet.
The lovable ladies are lots of fun,
And I meet them at dusk when my work is done,
For an evening without one is terribly tame
To a man who delights in a winsome dame.

  Oh, the frolicking, rollicking lassies-O.
To see them I never need glasses-O.
I'm never without 'em. There's something about 'em,
These frolicking, rollicking lassies-O.

I start for my work in the early morn,
With the sleep in my eye, and I feel forlorn,
When there, in a window, a lassie I see,
And she coyly and coaxingly winks at me.
The drowsiness speedily leaves my eye.
I throw back my shoulders and pass her by,
But not till I give her the wee little sign
That I'll call in the evening at half past nine.

Oh, the rollicking, frolicking lassies-O.
To see them I never need glasses-O.
They're velvety, very, and all to the merry,
These rollicking, frolicking lassies-O.

Although at the present I'm in my prime,
I suppose in the future there'll come a time
When I shall be sporting the lingering step
And shall have to admit that I've lost my pep.
But while I'm still young and my blood has tone,
It's no use to be spending my time alone;
So I think that I'll call on a rollicking wren
Who'll be looking for me about half past ten.

Oh, the rollicking, frolicking lassies-O.
To see them I never need glasses-O.
They're classy and clever. I'll love 'em forever,
These rollicking, frolicking lassies-O.

THE GARDEN

When the sun has sent the snowdrifts on their disappearing way,
And the balmy springtime breezes seem as tho they're here to stay,
When the ground is soft and mellow with the surface nice and dry,
Then we start to plant our garden, and I'll tell the reasons why.
First of all, the call of nature comes a-creeping up our spines,
As we hear the frogs a-croaking, one of springtime's surest signs
That the killing frosts are over and it's safe to plant the seeds
To insure a vast abundance for our vitaminous needs.
First we plow the garden deeply, and the fertilizer spread,
Then the harrow does the mixing, for the plantlets must be fed,
While the roller and the marker bring the job right up to date,
Soothing out the lumps and wrinkles, making rows all nice and straight.
Now we plant the early cabbage and the radishes and peas,

While the sun necessitates our stripping down to B.V.D.'s.
Oh, that genial warmth is luscious and we caper 'round and sing,
As the beets and chard and lettuce start a-growing in the spring.
Later on the corn and melons, beans and spinach and the cukes,
Plus the other things are planted with expectancy deluxe.
But we have to watch for cutworms, bugs and beetles and the weeds,
Or we'd miss the golden harvest that to satisfaction leads.
Yes, it's fine to have a garden. It's a good investment, too,
For the Protestant, the Catholic, the Gentile, and the Jew.
Nothing's ever stale and moldy, everything so fresh and clean,
While the profits of the middleman become extremely lean.
It is great to have the rhubarb, and a classy strawberry patch,
While asparagus in season will be rather hard to match.
These delicious garden products furnish vitamins galore.
All we have to do is pick 'em right outside the cottage door.

GEORGE WASHINGTON

Little George, I've heard it mentioned,
Had a daddy well-intentioned
And a mother who insisted that her son should tell the truth.
But one morning daddy stumbled
On some cherry chips and grumbled
That he guessed he knew who did it and reproved his erring youth.

Little George, a manly fellow
Who possessed no streak of yellow,
Spoke these words so oft repeated, "Dad, I cannot tell a lie.
Though I knew that I would catch it
I unsheathed my little hatchet,
And I chopped that precious cherry, so we'll have no cherry pie."

George was very energetic.
He was also quite athletic.
He could box and he could wrestle. He could ride the meanest roan,
And he loved to hear them holler
When he threw a silver dollar
Clear across the broad Potomac where it bounded off a stone.

George was once a public weigher
And an excellent surveyor.
As a soldier he was aces; as a leader he excelled.

Though his armies lacked nutrition,
He procured the ammunition
And by constant exhortation saved the day when they rebelled.

In our hectic Revolution
George preserved the Constitution
By declaring to the people that our freedom was the prize.
He was neither scared nor skittish,
And he licked those blooming British
And established in this nation freedom from all foreign ties.

Then a President was needed,
And, as George's skill exceeded
That of any other person, he was chosen for the plan.
As the leader of our nation
He won out by acclamation,
And the world has since acknowledged that our George was quite a man.

THE GOBULO

Dear children, have you ever heard about the Gobulo
That used to roam upon the earth ten thousand years ago?
There may be some of you who've heard about the monster bold,
But all the rest who haven't, why, I think you should be told,
Because, perhaps, the time may come when he will find a way
To climb once more upon the earth and see the light of day;
And if he should, we might as well within the ocean dive;
He'd surely catch us one by one and swallow us alive.

This awful, fearful Gobulo was forty-five feet high,
And just above his ugly nose he had one gleaming eye,
Which shone so brightly in the dark, 'twas just as light as day
All 'round about for miles and miles, a wonderful display.
One massive leg was all he had on which to stomp around,
But when he'd hop a hundred yards, 'twould fairly shake the ground.
And, oh! such arms and hooky hands. They'd surely make you gasp.
He'd swallow whole whoever chanced to come within his grasp.

This Gobulo had roamed at will through every land and clime;
The people knew not when he'd come and trembled all the time.
And so at last they all declared this monster must be slain;
So presently they hit upon a plan that seemed quite plain.
They dug a hole four thousand miles straight down into the earth.

'Twas very near, but just outside, the little town of Perth,
And when completed was the job, upon the hole they placed
A cover made of slender poles, and grass and leaves and waste.

You see, a man who didn't know about the hole at all
Would step upon this cover trap, and down the hole would fall.
And so they waited, knowing well, that soon the Gobulo
Would come along and feast on them, before he'd onward go.
But years and years of dread and fear had made these people wise—
They knew his eye would ferret out a crowd of any size.
And so they gathered 'round the trap for many a day and night,
Expecting every moment that the brute would come in sight.

But nothing happened, and they feared their work was all in vain,
When suddenly a well-known sound came rolling o'er the plain.
The Gobulo was coming on. They saw his wicked eye.
They knew that if he missed the trap, a part of them must die.
The gleam from out that fearful eye was streaming on ahead;
The Gobulo was hungry now and wanted to be fed.
'Twas plain he saw the huddled bunch of toothsome maids and men;
Perhaps he'd think the circle was a human slaughter pen.

On! On! he came; another leap, success or failure meant.
He made the leap and fair and square within the circle went.
A smash! A crash! And down that hole the monster disappeared.
And upward from that fearful place came sounds both wild and weird.
Next day the people filled the hole wherein the giant fell,
But science says the Gobulo is still alive and well.
It says he's in the center of the earth whereon we live,
And maybe he'll get out again and lots of trouble give.

To prove the fact that he's alive, they say on winter nights,
He shoots the streamers from his eye, which make the northern lights.
For all the big volcanoes that are spouting fire and flame,
The scientists are all agreed the Gobulo's to blame.
And when the thunder rolls and rolls, and lightning flashes hiss,
It's safe to say the Gobulo is causing all of this.
So, children dear, when earthquakes shake the earth from pole to pole,
The Gobulo may scramble up a crooked earthquake hole.

And so you see, you girls and boys must keep in fighting trim,
For if the Gobulo comes back, your chances may be slim.
He'll eat the naughty children first—they have a spicy taste—
So start right now to mend your ways; you have no time to waste!

GRADUATION THOUGHTS

We've assembled tonight in this famous old hall
To receive our diplomas, that we in the fall
May enter the high school, imposing and grand,
And wonderful things for ourselves we have planned.

We have spent many years in achieving this goal,
But we've just made a start in our climb up the knoll.
It's a hard, weary grind, but we've slipped into high;
If we keep the straight path, we'll arrive by and by.

The high school, of course, is a wonderful stride,
And college comes next with the doors open wide,
And those who survive and come through with acclaim
Will surely be fitted for fortune and fame.

And then, in the future, we'll strike such a gait
That it's probable quite we shall all become great.
How proud you will feel to look back on tonight
And remember these classmates all trembling with fright.

Dear teachers, we'll miss you; you'll see us again.
We shall all try to prove you've not labored in vain.
As years travel onward, and upward we go,
We promise due credit on you to bestow.

Dear people, we're glad of this wonderful chance.
Your faces are kindly, we see at a glance.
And when through the high school with credit we've passed,
You'll notice a chance in us, pleasing and vast.

THE GRASSHOPPER

A grasshopper, sunning himself on a stalk,
Composure and comfort suggesting,
Gave neighborhood insects occasion to talk,
Concerning his posture while resting.

The gnat, a decidedly delicate dame,
Adroitly maneuvered a landing,
And joining the others was heard to exclaim,
"I'm sure the old fellow is standing."

The butterfly noting the grasshopper's pose
While stealthily over him flitting,
Alighting, proceeded at once to disclose
The fact that he thought he was sitting.

Then grandfather beetle deserted his oak
And came to the contest a-trotting.
He drew a long breath and with confidence spoke,
"I know the old duffer is squatting."

The cricket tiptoed to the grasshopper's side
And said in a way most appealing,
"Do you stand, sit, or squat?"
And the hopper replied,
"I'm kneeling, my friend; yes, I'm kneeling."

The ant, by all standards the wisest of all,
The views of the others defying,
Profoundly declared in his usual drawl,
"I am firmly convinced that he's lying."

THE GRINDSTONE

Go round, you imp of Satan. Do your stuff.
Your sham at work is nothing but a bluff.

My leg is numb and feels no part of me,
And I may soon have water on the knee.

Your grit cuts slower than the sands of Time;
Your lesser fault is that of pantomime.

Your putty face slides underneath this axe
And leaves upon its edge few telltale tracks.

That's right, go backwards. Undo what you've done.
Do you suppose I'm turning you for fun?

Go round there frontwards, you ungrateful rock.
You should have stayed a solid, sandstone block.

The man who had the nerve to quarry you
Would rate as captain of a pirate crew.

The man who cut a grindstone from your mass
Should rot six feet beneath hog-trodden grass.

Your bearings squeak beneath your sodden weight
And seem to voice discouragement and hate.

I'll swear by saline sweat upon my brow
You'd be a perfect anchor for a scow.

GUB-GUB

Across the hot Saymarzo sands
The giant gub-gub bimbly beeps.
He snaws the maultus avocands
And bauperates the squingy squeaps.

With mure resending ummerbaugh
His maxtrous alks are raminous,
While fleeds at Ober-Ammergau
Defungulate the shaminous.

HANDLING THE HEN

In every business enterprise in which the people join,
That they may most successful be in corralling the coin,
They find that all is not serene, and obstacles they meet,
Which must be overcome before they enter easy street.
The moguls toil from morn till night, inducing friend or foe
To buy their wares that they may make another bunch of dough.
They advertise their watered stock, and take the people's cash,
That they may lunch on sirloin steak, and shun the chophouse hash.
It's just a few who ride around in heated limousines;
The rest of all humanity are munching pork and beans.
But all this inequality can now be counted out—
The heralded Utopia is here without a doubt.
No longer can the moneyed class encompass all outdoors;
No more can they the apples eat and pass around the cores.
No more can grasping sharks secure each kopeck, sou, and yen;
The secret lies in modern ways of handling the hen.
The hen, I say, that lowly bird is wealth personified;
She only needs a gentle push to be our joy and pride.
She holds within her feathered frame a fortune vast and grand;
With proper food and gentle care she'll shell to "beat the band."
You'll never see the time again when eggs will plenty be;
Their mission makes of them right now a stern necessity.

81

They're eaten by the multitude, from millionaires to yeggs.
Who'd ever think of breakfast now without the luscious eggs?
As long ago as Noah's time fresh eggs were much renowned;
Within the Ark ten thousand birds were laying all around,
And Shem and Ham and Japheth each would start and bring them in.
They must have tasted pretty fair to Noah's kith and kin.
And where would Crusoe now have been if eggs had given out?
Without the eggs the packer's plans would all be put to rout.
I tell you, eggs have come to stay; so don't discard my plea.
Get in the swing and play the game and meet prosperity.
If anyone is skeptical and doubts my proffered words,
Just meet a man whose specialty is prize Rhode Island birds.
You'll find he owns a neat coupe; his face is wreathed in smiles.
He'll show you eggs of late design in stacks and heaps and piles.
He'll say he likes Rhode Island Reds, and also Plymouth Rocks;
He'll say that breed amounts to less than caring for the flocks.
So if you wish to start the game and learn the proper grips,
Just visit a good poultry man and get some worthwhile tips.

HAPPY MEDIUM

A pretty little maiden girl once took a wedding jump.
She hooked up with a gentleman and got an awful bump.
He was so good and kind and true it gave her fearful pains.
He died of grief, and, therefore, she cremated his remains.

She put his ashes in a jug, which on the mantle stood,
Then started out to find a man who wasn't quite so good.
This time she hooked up with a gent who'd traveled all the routes
Which lead from good to bad to worse, by way of bats and toots.

If the ponds were made of whiskey, and the ocean made of rum,
He'd drink them dry and put the whales and fishes on the bum.
So now she thinks she'd rather have a hubby dead as nails
Than a husky live one breezing in with cyclones in his sails.

The moral of this little rhyme is very plain, you see.
The very good and very bad are just for you and me,
Because the happy medium, as you will surely find,
The other girl has captured with a lasso, from behind.

THE HERMIT

The hermit resides on the mountain.
His cabin is staunch in the gale.
His bubbling spring, like a fountain,
Flows ceaselessly down to the vale.

The sun and the moon are his cronies,
The stars and the planets his friends.
He loses no time on the ponies;
No sporting events he attends.

The hermit has higher ambitions.
He admires Henry David Thoreau.
He thinks nature's magicians
Are butterfly, rabbit, and crow.

The quest for more knowledge excites him,
On bobcat or beaver or bear.
His out-of-doors nature invites him
To visit the porcupine's lair.

He jots down his findings completely,
Later on to be read by mankind.
They're classified clearly and neatly
And finally legibly signed.

In time there will come recognition
What a true nature-lover has done.
Some hermit extended a mission
That David Thoreau had begun.

We'll wait for that hermit's disclosure
Of secrets in nature's domain,
And learn from his masterly dossier
His facts gleaned by sun, moon, and rain.

HERO OF THE MISSISSIPPI FLOOD

When the raging Mississippi overflowed the countryside,
Spreading death and desolation through the region far and wide,
There were many thrilling rescues as the flood went sweeping by,
But a certain southern planter made a record none deny.

Swirling waters, floating hazards sent no terror to his soul,
As his flatboat skimmed the torrent at the guidance of his pole.
Men and women, little children, from those waters black with mud
Were delivered by the hero of the Mississippi flood.

In the evenings by the fireside he delighted one and all
By recounting his adventures in that fearful water fall,
But the rheumatism got him and he died a hero's death
And proceeded up to heaven with the flood upon his breath.

With admission on his record as a savior of mankind
He was granted great attention and was duly wined and dined,
And his sojourn there in heaven would have proved a perfect plan,
If perchance he hadn't mentioned something to a certain man.

He was speaking to Saint Peter. "Will you kindly let me know
Who's that thoughtful-looking gentleman with locks as white as snow?
I was speaking to him lately of my Mississippi plight,
When I saved so many people on that dark and dismal night.

"I described the raging waters and the billows and the spray,
How I pushed the flatboat forward, and he rudely walked away.
Do you see the man I mention? He is standing by that door."
"Yes," Saint Peter calmly answered, "I can see him. That is Noah."

HIS CHOICE

He journeyed North, East, South, and West,
    This man of taste and wealth,
To ascertain the region best
    For business, pleasure, health.

At California's golden strand
    He gave a searching gaze,
But business in that western land
    Was huddled in a haze.

He rambled on to Oregon
    And met the tourist flocks.
The things he chiefly gazed upon
    Were Rocky Mountain rocks.

From Colorado's towering heights
    He viewed the grand La Platte.
His eyes admired the gorgeous sights,
    But who could live on that?

Across the level Kansas plains
    He took a hurried hop
With views from observation trains
    And didn't even stop.

To Florida he made his way
    And met some charming folk.
Both kind and courteous were they,
    Though most of them were broke.

He scanned the Adirondack peaks,
    The foothills and the slopes,
Exploring round for weeks and weeks
    With naught but blasted hopes.

At last to fair New England's charms
    He doffed his dusty hat.
He saw the cities and the farms
    And pondered this and that.

He journeyed North, East, South, and West;
    I'll say he did, and how!
New England met the final test,
    And he's our neighbor now.

HOPE

A wealthy old banker,
    Unmarriedly tragic,
Began late to hanker
    For marital magic.

An heir for his money
    Seemed sensibly proper;
He courted a "Honey"
    Who labeled him "Poppa."

He clothed her in ermine,
    But said, "Ere they mate us,
I wish to determine
    My physical status."

He called on Doc Wizzie,
    Of wide reputation,
Who gave him a physical
    Examination.

Said Doc, "I'm not blinded,
    And, since you've petitioned,
I find you're heir-minded,
    But not heir-conditioned."

HORSE TRADE

Old Deacon Van Winkle was pious and plain.
He came to our town from a village in Maine.
He had a big horse that was fuzzy and fat,
Whose coat was the color of that of a bat.

One morning Si Skinner drove up in a gig.
The deacon came out in his clerical rig.
"Do you ever swap horses?" Si asked with a grin.
"Oh, yes," said the deacon, "that ain't any sin."

The deacon then trotted Bucephalus out.
Si looked him all over for spavins and gout.
Si's horse was just fair but appeared to be sound.
The deacon climbed in and they trotted him 'round.

Arrived at the barn they got down to brass tacks.
Said Si, "This here hoss has been raced at the tracks.
His mark I forget but he's able to step;
Just feed him good oats and he'll show you the pep."

"Bucephalus, here, has a-plenty of fizz.
A blind man could see what a critter he is.
He don't look very good. He's a powerful brute."
Said the deacon, "I'll swap for a hundred to boot."

Si argued and fumed but the deacon stood pat.
Si wanted a horse that was massive and fat.
"I'll give you just ninety, although I am bled."
The deacon's eyes twinkled. "We'll shift 'em," he said.

They shifted the horses and Si drove away,
But mad as could be he returned the next day.
He yelled at the deacon and made a great fuss.
"This hoss is stone blind, you deceitful old cuss."

The deacon developed a scowl a mile wide,
And said to Si Skinner, "Don't tell me I lied;
You are tryin' to squeal and I reckoned you would.
I told you the truth; he don't look very good."

HYGIENE

Two men were conversing one day on the street;
    The weather was sultry and hot.
No shade cooled the breeze and the terrible heat
    Would have wilted both men on the spot,
But not so with these. They were tougher than steel;
    They had studied hygiene by the bale
And couldn't make out how a fellow could feel
    Any other than hearty and hale.

"Just think," argued one, "I was flat on the shelf.
    The doctors all called it a strain.
But I finally won by convincing myself
    'Twas a tooth that was causing my pain.
I figured my chances; without any doubt,
    I was out of the game for a spell—
So I propped up my courage and had the thing out,
    And now I am perfectly well."

"I know," said the other. "See that and see that,"
    And he opened his mouth half a mile.
"The blasted lumbago had walloped me flat;
    I expected to die for a while.
My dentist demurred and declared it a shame,
    To sacrifice teeth that are sound.
But I knew and demanded he pull just the same,
    And now I am tough as a hound."

Just then an old codger came shuffling along.
    He balanced himself on a cane.
It was really quite evident something was wrong.
    His facial expression showed pain.
His coat was too thick for the time of the year,
    And a sweater appeared underneath.
"How's that for a case?" said one hygienic seer,
    "And all that's at fault are his teeth."

"I know," said the other. "Let's tell him the truth;
    We'll soon have him happy and gay."
"My man, for acquiring perpetual youth,
    Pull out all your teeth right away."
The sufferer grunted and scornfully said,
    With a look that was clammy and cold,
"Not a tooth of my own have I had in my head,
    Since the day I was ninety years old."

One listener whispered, "I think we're all wrong,
    Good neighbor, our chances are slim.
If he can hit ninety and hobble along,
    We would better get pointers from him."
"My man, will you tell us the secret you hold
    In sharing longevity's plan?
We judge you are nearly one hundred years old,
    A truly remarkable man."

Said he, "That's a secret I've held with my wife;
    I cannot now give it away.
I've kept it profoundly the most of my life;
    Our years have been fruitful and gay.
And, though you are both intellectual men,
    I'm willing to hazard a guess:
I'll place quite a wager at twenty to ten
    I can trim you at checkers or chess."

I CALLS UPON MY LADY LOVE

I calls upon my lady love;
She meets me at the gate.
"Good evening, dear," I says to her.
"I fear I'm rather late.

"I stopped to see a friend of mine,
A good old pal is SHE.
I couldn't make her understand,
And so I'm late, you see."

And then the fireworks started;
We very nearly parted,
As down the street I darted, quick,
But she's too quick for me.

She grabs me by the collar
And chokes me till I holler,
And then takes every dollar slick,
Before she sets me free.

I gets my necktie straightened out;
She says that I'm a brute.
When I reply, she pivots 'round
And bings me on the snoot.

It's mighty hard to love a gal
Who has such stunning ways,
But then I guess they're all the same
These flipper flapper days.

I used to be a scrapper;
So in my arms I wrap her,
And say, "You little flapper dear;
I want you to be mine."

And then she tried to fist me,
But luckily she missed me,
And then she up and kissed me—here!
Now everything is fine.

Soon after that the parson comes
And does his little bit;
We hire a flat upon the flat,
But I'm as flat as it.

The landlord comes a-snooping 'round
To gather in the rent;
So out we go because, you see,
I didn't have a cent.

I really am a goner;
We stand upon the corner.
I'd really like to pawn her,
But I know that she would kick.

She grabs a passing poodle
And swings him on my noodle
To the tune of Yankee Doodle,
But the time is double quick.

I rubs the spots the poodle hits
And then pulls out a claw;
I fear that hydrophobia
May settle in my jaw.

My darling wife is holding up
A telegraphic pole.
She seems to think without her help
'Twill vanish down the hole.

And then she spies her popper.
I tries but cannot stop her.
She makes him call a copper band,
Which promptly runs me in.

They shoves me in a cell-o
Where lives another fellow.
His countenance is yellow,
And his name is Charlie Chin.

"Hello," says I to Charlie Chin,
"What puts you on the blink?"
Says he, "I meets a Yankee girl
And gives a little wink.

"The Yankee girl, she grabs a brick
And slams me on the mush;
So down I goes and wallows 'round
Among the slimy slush.

"I can't do any thinkin';
My eyes are scarcely blinkin'.
The coppers think I'm drinkin';
So they puts me in for life."

"Who is this female Yankee?"
Says I, which makes Chin cranky.
And when he says, "Ann Hanky,"
Then I knows it is my wife.

"But how did you become to know
Ann Hanky, Charlie Chin?"
"She brings her popper's laundry down,"
Says Charlie with a grin.

"But now she's married to a bum,
The worst you've ever seen.
And if she catches him asleep,
She'll break his bummy bean."

Next morning, bright and early,
A great big bouncing burly,
With visage sour and surly,
Comes and fumbles with the keys.

I takes a dry martino,
Then leaves San Bernadino,
And makes my way to Reno.
O - - - H! It's lovely to be free!

I DOFF MY HAT

I rolled along the county pike at thirty miles an hour.
My dear old bus was full of pep with classy speed and power.
New piston rings I had installed. From carbon she was free.
New patent sparkplugs furnished juice, each costing me a V.

A sense of independence filled and satisfied my mind.
No longer I'd be humbly forced to trail along behind.
I let her out another notch. She jumped and shot ahead.
"I never knew she had such speed," unto myself I said.

The shimmering trees sped swiftly by, or so to me it seemed.
I'd never so contented felt, excepting when I dreamed.
But then a purring sound I heard. I gave a backward glance.
A fellow in a brand-new car! Oh, baby, what a chance!

I gripped the wheel at forty per. We then were side by side.
Another notch to forty-five, but still as one we glide.
I set the spark ahead and pressed the throttle to the floor
But could not shake that purring car at sixty-three or four.

The driver of that speedy car then motioned me to stop.
With dire forebodings I foresaw a session with a cop.
I slowly slackened speed and tried my best to hide my wrath,
And then to make the matter worse he turned across my path.

Abruptly I applied the brakes. His car backed up a bit.
The driver turned his head to speak. I nearly had a fit.
In pure disgust his accents fell, enshrouded in a sigh,
"Please tell me, mister, how to shift from second into high."

IF I WERE RICH

If I were rich I'll tell you what I'd do right off the bat.
I'd buy a brand-new outfit for each kid; I'll tell you that.
And wifey should have gorgeous clothes, all spick-and-span and new,
And all the latest furniture would soon come into view.

If I were rich we'd entertain our neighbors every night
And have the auto painted up in colors dazzling bright.
I'd put new carpets on the floors and frescoe every wall.
I'd circulate the money winter, summer, spring, and fall.

If I were rich! For Heaven's Sake! I blush at what I say!
I'm the richest man in fifty states, in every *worthwhile* way.
I have my wife and children dear, all true to Uncle Sam.
I guess they'd rather take a chance with me just as I am.

ILL WIND

The Marquis Bozarro, a soldierly runt,
Had shouldered his rifle and gone to the front.
The Marchioness cherished his lingering hug
And wept till a puddle appeared on the rug.

An athletic Duke, on the hoof six feet two,
Arrived just in time for a friendly adieu,
And, noting her ladyship's evident grief,
Remained to administer righteous relief.

His infinite tact and his masculine charm
Succeeded in quelling her grievous alarm.
Said he, "Though the Marquis is now on the spot,
I'll bet even-up that he doesn't get shot."

She glanced at the marvelous man at her side,
Compared with the one who had made her his bride.
"And when is your furlough to end?" queried she.
"One week from tomorrow I'm leaving," said he.

The weather was chill and her ladyship then
Suggested a walk in her favorite glen.
Across the broad acres that bordered a rill,
Together they sped to the foot of a hill.

Said she, as he aided her over a fence,
"Let's seek out a spot where the shadows are dense."
Then reasoned the Duke as they entered the wood,
It's an ill wind, indeed, that blows nobody good.

ILLUSIONS

At midnight I stood on the deck. The clock was striking two.
Electric cars came streaming by upon the ocean blue.
The sea gulls walked upon the fog, and, following their tracks,
The hound fish came in such pursuit the scent was at their backs.

The sales upon the sailing boats were advertised aloud.
The sun beamed on the auctioneer, the daughter on the crowd.
The whales and sharks and cuttlefish were having quite a spree.
The rubifoam from off their wings was falling in the sea.
The little minnows won by chance the mermaids one by one.
And after dark they'd sit and dance beneath the blazing sun.
The sea was calm. The dashing waves were rolling o'er and o'er.
They rolled upon a little clam and crushed him on the shore.
When they returned, the undertow contracted quite a corn,
And lost its nail, and all swelled up. It surely looked forlorn.
The night was dark, the stars were bright, the sailors came in view.
The dipper joggled upside down and drenched them through and
    through.
A pretty mermaid dancing by had dressed herself with care.
She gathered up some little waves and put them in her hair.
A bunch of swordfish came from lunch; they still were wearing bibs.
They pushed their swords into the ships right in between their ribs.
The ships were tickled half to death; they nearly split their sides.
Then laughed and giggled half the night, wrapped snugly in the tides.
The lobsters and the lobsterettes were waltzing on the spray.
They had a little moonshine still, and so were feeling gay.
And then they danced the minuet between the drys and wets.
They lost their pipes and had to smoke their seaweed cigarettes.

THE INDEPENDENT FARMER (1)

The independent farmer is a man of sterling worth;
We cannot do without him, for he cultivates the earth.
He hustles 'round from morn till night and takes his pay in praise,
For everyone shows pure delight in crops the farmers raise.
He starts out in the early spring and plows a lot of ground,
Then fertilizer spreads and plants the seedlets by the pound.
He fights the bugs and beetles till his frame is like a rail;
He's about as independent as a bubble in a gale.

The independent farmer when his crop of hay is made
Is toiling in the blazing sun at ninety in the shade.
And when his hay is nicely cured without a drop of rain
A thunder shower soaks it so he spreads it out again.
And then the hailstones come along and cut his vines to shreds,
And slash his corn and cauliflower and punch his cabbage heads.
So when he strolls around the farm to take a worried look,
He's about as independent as a fishworm on a hook.

The independent farmer when the harvest time is near
Begins to brighten up a bit and smile from ear to ear,
But while his choice tomatoes are a-ripening on the vine
The price of choice tomatoes takes a sharp and swift decline.
The phosphate bills are coming in. The taxes must be paid.
He doesn't have a lot of time to ramble in the shade.
So hustling over to the bank another loan to beg,
He's about as independent as a chicken in an egg.

But when the winter comes around he hasn't much to do,
Except to bring the year's supply of fuel into view.
The days are short and so he starts and stops by lantern light.
He saws and splits the sturdy trees from morning until night.
But in the evening by the fire his work is at an end.
He spends his time because his time is all he has to spend.
He leads a very varied life; he toils and slaves and works.
He's about as independent as a Greek among the Turks.

THE INDEPENDENT FARMER (2)

The independent farmer is a man we all admire.
Though life is hard, he plans to raise the food that we require.
He rises early, works all day, and when the evening comes,
He scarcely has sufficient pep to sit and twirl his thumbs.
The springtime work comes with a rush; the plowing must be done,
And fertilizer spread before the planting has begun.
He plants the tiny seedlets till his arm is like a crank.
He's about as independent as a turtle in a tank.

The independent farmer in the glorious summertime
Is plastered over, head to foot, with sticky mud and grime.
The dust that drifts across the field, combined with sprayer juice,
Clogs up his eyes and sweating pores and pries his temper loose.
The bugs and beetles multiply. The weeds are in the gain.
Despite the never-ending spray the blight is raising Cain.
The poor, old farmer springs a sigh and nearly passes out.
He's about as independent as a cricket in a trout.

The independent farmer when the harvest time is near,
Instead of feeling jubilant, uncorks a bitter tear.
The market shows an upward trend with prices in the "pink."
He hoped for these, but what's the use? His crops are on the blink.

94

At first the drought had come along and shriveled up the ground,
And then a flood descended and his crops were nearly drowned;
And when he strolls around the farm that put him in the hole,
He's about as independent as a bedbug in a bowl.

The independent farmer when the winter comes along
Has many hours and days and weeks to figure up what's wrong.
He sees his banker for a loan, already in arrears,
To tide him over till another bunch of bugs appears.
The fluffy, downy snowflakes swirl before the zero blast.
The farmer hustles in the wood and prays that it will last.
With taxes high and income low his inner thoughts rebel.
He's about as independent as a lightning bug in hell.

INDICTMENT

We know that war's grim aftermath
    Is causing much distress,
And children tread the wayward path
    That leads to lawlessness.

To think these children are to blame
    Is idle, false, absurd,
And parenthood should writhe in shame
    At what is seen and heard.

Good precepts set for girls and boys
    By parents, young and old,
Would pave the way for greater joys
    Than crime could ever hold.

Few children would be led astray,
    If mother's love be shared.
Delinquency would fade away,
    If fathers only cared.

INDISPENSABLE

A farmer had a special hoe, exceptionally crude. Eleven years he'd
used that hoe to keep the weeds subdued. He foolishly admired that
hoe, the only one he had, a sort of family affair—he'd used it as a lad.
At last it bent and splintered up, its fate forever sealed. He bought a

brand-new shiny hoe and hastened to the field. It had the old one trimmed a mile; he told his neighbors so. Good people, there is no such thing as an indispensable hoe.

A business baron owned a farm, the outcome of a dream. He kept a brindle mooley-cow to furnish milk and cream. Eleven years he'd kept that cow for sentimental sake and also for the cottage cheese like mother used to make. This cow had never strained herself to fill production's cup, but still she'd make baloney and that's where she ended up. A real fine cow then took her place, and is he joyous now? Good people, there is no such thing as an indispensable cow.

A gentleman past middle life possessed a family car. Eleven years he'd babied it on journeys near and far. He'd readjust transmission bands and tinker with the spark. It filled his very soul with hope to hear the engine bark. Now that was all the car he had to last till Judgment Day, but suddenly it folded like the poet's "One-Hoss Shay." He bought a modern chariot that didn't jump or jar. Good people, there is no such thing as an indispensable car.

A giant corporation had encountered many a squall. It had a man as manager who thought he knew it all. Eleven years he'd held the reins and cracked the driver's whip and watched with keen alacrity his menials hop and skip. Although he'd not admit that they were losing their esteem, his underlings exploded and protested his regime. They saw their chance to turn him out and try a saner plan. Good people, there is no such thing as an indispensable man.

INSURANCE ADJUSTER

The insurance adjuster, as you are aware,
 Must tackle his job with the greatest of care.
No slips or mistakes are allowed to creep in
 To bother the boss or the sorrowing kin.
The record of each individual case
 Must state with precision the time and the place.
Perchance there are witnesses, names and address
 Must all be recorded but never by guess.
The clever adjuster must know all the dope,
 The track of a tire or the strength of a rope,
The cost of false teeth and the value of pain,
 The rules of the road from Missouri to Maine,

The female appeal or the cost of a dress,
    A barrel of anguish, a ton of distress.
In fact, he must know all the answers to date,
    Thus tempting the boss not to give him the gate.
The cagey adjuster must rate as a seer,
    Profound in his reasoning, calmly severe,
Pretending to favor the injured's appeal,
    And all the while scheming a double-cross deal.
His firm pays him money for doing just that.
    He'll settle a case at the drop of a hat,
Because with a jury you never can tell—
    Apparently clever, they're dumber than . . . anything.
The honest adjuster has lofty desires,
    But what can he do when he's dealing with liars?
The ambulance chasers are there in a flash,
    Before the adjuster has heard of the crash.
The adjuster assumes a responsible place,
    Well burdened with care and a smile on his face.
His pay is so high he has plenty to spare,
    And he'll soon be retiring, a proud millionaire.

INTUITION

Intuition. Woman claims it:
    Says it isn't elsewhere found.
But I claim, and proof will offer,
    That it's scattered all around.

Now take Jonah for example.
    His would seem a hopeless lot.
Intuition, pure and simple,
    Solved his problems on the spot.

Just what makes the bedbug classy?
    Bedbug brains are dull and slow.
He's endowed with intuition,
    For he knows just where to go.

So you see that intuition
    Not alone in woman rests,
Tho we must admit she's clever,
    When it comes to hubby's guests.

INVESTIGATION
BY MYSTICAL PROPHET

The mystical Prophet, abounding in gall,
Once summoned the planets to make him a call.
He wished to determine if life through the years
Could really exist on the heavenly spheres.
Then Mercury, Jupiter, Saturn, and Mars
Abruptly abandoned their neighboring stars
And heeding the summons advanced to the test,
But Venus declined to unite with the rest.

However, the Prophet with infinite zeal
Discovered conditions which proved to reveal
The fact that on Saturn no life could exist;
So his thoughts on that planet were quickly dismissed.
Now Jupiter's status was somewhat obscure—
No atmosphere present, of that he was sure,
But he found a thin fog and was soon to affirm
That it couldn't sustain a pneumonia germ.

Then poor little Mercury, silent and shy,
Came under the oracle's critical eye.
Its shell was so rough and devoid of all charm,
The oracle, backing away in alarm,
Turned quickly to Mars, a more promising quest,
And thoroughly gave her the miracle test.
But, as with the others, he labored in vain;
No life could exist minus humus and rain.

Since Venus preferred isolation to fame,
The Prophet portrayed her a diffident dame.
He reasoned perchance she had moisture and air,
All manner of life might be flourishing there.
He thought her refusal to answer his plea
Denoted the fact that undoubtedly she
Was loath to divulge any intimate news
Concerning her private advancement or views.

They sat there in silence and gazed at the score.
There suddenly came a loud knock on the door.
The planets, disturbed by the terrible din,
Departed in haste to return to their kin.
The door opened slowly, the Moon then appeared.

A voice from a man with a flowing, white beard
Boomed out: "Though it's small like a captive balloon,
You might like to know there's a man in the moon."

IT'S MAPLE SUGAR TIME

Well, the maple sap is dripping and we're really on the beam,
With the sugarhouse enveloped in a cloud of gushing steam,
As the tractor, moving slowly through the piles of drifting snow,
Keeps the sap tanks well replenished with a never-ending flow.
Oh, the sugarhouse is cozy when the air outside is chill—
As that caterpillar tractor comes a-chugging up the hill
With its precious load of sweetness that will soon be boiled away
Into maple syrup candy, making everybody gay.

The maple syrup season is a time for extra toil—
But our nerves are all aquiver when the sap begins to boil,
For we know from past experience we'll hear a joyous shout,
When the luscious maple syrup comes a-flowing from the spout.
By a long-established custom, maple syrup takes its place
As the very choicest sweetness to delight the human race.
From no other source in nature comes a product so replete
With delectable provisions for an epicurean treat.

It's hustle, hustle, hustle now from morning, noon, and night.
We have to boil it speedily to make the syrup light.
Our constant aim is cleanliness to keep the product pure.
With each container sterilized we're absolutely sure.
This maple syrup industry is really broad and vast.
The maple sugar angle has attraction unsurpassed.
No nectar known to all mankind, this whole wide world around,
Can equal maple products by the gallon or the pound.

From the great St. Lawrence River to our own Long Island shore,
Scattered over hills and valleys there are maple trees galore.
Farmers tap them by the millions; sugar camps become aglow,
As the trailers, trucks, and tractors wend their journeys through the snow.
Many mortgages are lifted, many debts are yearly paid
From the sale of maple products of the very highest grade.
All New England is the winner when it deftly turns the key,
Which releases untold riches from the sugar maple tree.

JACK

When Jack figured up he had money to spare,
He married a girl who was shapely and fair.
His gift of a gem in a setting of jade
Placed the gorgeous Hope diamond far in the shade.

With his wife in the car 'round the country he rolled.
They stopped at a college not gifted with gold.
He made a short speech which was welcomed with glee—
"Here's a bunch of long green; have a chapel on me."

They paraded in nighties and shouted his name.
They made him a Doctor to add to his fame.
Still Little Jack Horner emerged from the scene
With a number six hat and a neckband eighteen.

They called on more colleges, hospitals too.
He always shelled out and his prominence grew.
And so he became, when he'd finished his fun,
A Doctor of everything under the sun.

A trip to his home, to his Mother and Dad,
Brought tears to their eyes as they welcomed their lad,
And Ma and Pa's argument never abates
As to who takes the credit for Jack's clever traits.

But Jack, to himself, claims all credit is due
And mentions his reasons for holding that view.
He claims that he guided the progeny whirl
By pre-natal prayers that he'd not be a girl.

JIM AND I

Jim and I were simply sitting,
    Sitting on a short settee.
Jim was smoking. I was knitting.
    I was happy. So was he.

We were talking of our wedding,
    Which was soon to be a fact,
While he watched my needle threading
    In and out with graceful tact.

100

With a bandaged thumb, in braces,
    Sat a gloomy-looking guy.
"Broke his thumb in seven places,"
    Whispered Jimmy, drawing nigh.

Whispered I, "I'd now inquire
    How he chanced to break his thumb."
Jim replied, "He hollered, 'Fire,'
    In the language deaf and dumb."

JOE IS DEAD

Yes, Joe is dead, my youngest son,
An' farmin' now won't be much fun.
Joe was the strongest man, I vow,
That ever roped a kickin' cow.
He weighed three hundred on the hoof.
My hay scales weighed him; that's the proof.
He'd whirl a log above his head
An' slam it down upon the sled.

Yes, Joe is dead. I feel the loss.
I swear, I'd sooner lost a hoss.
It's tough in spring; there's lots to do,
An' I'd jest wintered Joey through.
I'd got him boots of cattle hide,
The size fourteen and extry wide.
My other boys would act like coots
A-sloshin' 'round in Joey's boots.

His maw took stock in Joey, too,
An' I don't know what she will do.
He'd eat the leavin's slick an' clean,
More perfect than I'd ever seen.
Pertater skins an' apple cores
An' sweepin's from the granary floors
He'd gobble up an' never clog,
An' now I'll have to get a hog.

It's awful hard to get ahead
When one you need is lyin' dead.
The other boys won't have no fun
To do the work that Joey done.

I wish, regarding Joey's case,
Another son could take his place.
But still I'll save a little dough;
They won't eat half as much as Joe.

JOE AND SAMANTHY

I

"It happened at a huskin' bee.
The lights was low; you couldn't see,
An' kissin' raged like all possessed.
I grabbed a girl like all the rest.
She give me quite a tussle there.
I gently stroked her wavy hair,
An' up there in that dusty loft
I found her mighty nice an' soft.

"Then mixed up in the kissin' game
She said Samanthy was her name.
I felt her glossy hair again
An' popped the question there an' then.
Next day I met her in the light
An' gosh, all hemlocks, what a sight!
She wore a gunny-sacksy gown;
One eye looked up, the other down.

"Her nose, a little on one side,
Was rather red an' extry wide.
She had a raft of moles an' warts
An' blemishes of other sorts.
Although mistakes I'd often made,
I'd never backed out in a trade.
I took Samanthy for my wife,
The greatest bargain of my life.

"I'm awful glad I failed to see
Samanthy at that huskin' bee.
An' now she always calls me 'Sir.'
Our children look like me, not her.
She ain't no cure for ailin' eyes,
But you should taste her pumpkin pies.
In every way she's stood the test.
I wouldn't swap her for Mae West."

102

"I'm awful glad we couldn't see
Each other at that huskin' bee.
The lights was low; the barn was dark,
An' kissin' made the brightest spark.
A feller grabbed me right away
An' took me up amongst the hay.
I'd never smelt a farmer's breath.
I thought he'd smother me to death.

"His arms had power like a vise,
An' I was feelin' awful nice.
I thought his name I'd ought to know
He said that I could call him Joe.
Well, Joe an' me was feelin' fine;
My hand in his, an' his in mine.
An' then he sprung the trap on me
An' said he'd pay the parson's fee.

"That kinder took me by surprise,
But twenty years had made me wise,
An' I had never had a beau
That pleased me quite so much as Joe.
An' so I didn't hem or haw,
But said to Joe his word was law.
An' that is how it come to be
That Joe, the farmer, married me.

"I know I ain't no Fairy Fay,
An' Joe discovered that next day,
But one thing I will let you know,
I've seen more handsome men than Joe,
But he's so nice an' kind an' square—
He's better than a millionaire.
An' here's the truthful, honest dope,
I wouldn't swap him for Bob Hope."

JOSEPHUS JAY

In Rochester, I've heard it said, there lived Josephus Jay.
    He was quite a man for gaiety and glee.
He was never known to grumble at his work or at his play.
    With his money he was frivolously free.

He liked to sing a jolly song while working on his job,
    And his voice was quite melodious and clear.
But the only song that he could sing was "Kernels on the Cob,"
    And in time it got to sounding rather queer.

Josephus never cared to fight; he'd rather walk away.
    And at certain times it's well to take a walk.
A big and burly southerner was feeling rather gay,
    And he sauntered up to have a little talk.
He heard Josephus sing the words of "*Colonels* on the Cob,"
    As he splashed the paint upon the wall of brick.
He squared away and placed a blow upon Josephus's knob,
    And Josephus's neck was broken like a stick.

They scraped him off the sidewalk and they propped him up in bed
    And they poured the whiskey down his broken neck.
The doctor came and told them that Josephus Jay was dead,
    And they all declared he was an awful wreck.
It's hard to kill a rubberneck—most people will agree—
    Which Josephus demonstrated very soon.
He started singing "Money Musk," but couldn't get the key;
    So he warbled up the same old kernel tune.

They found an ancient lightning rod and pushed it down his spine;
    Josephus writhed and wriggled up and down.
They pumped the brandy into him till Joe was feeling fine,
    And he hailed a cab and taxied into town.
Next morning he was on the job and gaily painting brick,
    But he kept his eyes a-roving round about.
He said the lightning rod had helped, but brandy did the trick,
    And his "Kernels on the Cob" came booming out.

JOSEPHUS JONES

Josephus Jones showed no delight
    When served with chophouse hash.
For such, at morning, noon, and night,
    He paid his hard-earned cash.
He visioned lamb or chops or veal
    And promptly mutineered.
He waited just another meal,
    But still the hash appeared.

Josephus Jones pushed back his chair.
    Disgust he plainly showed.
He rose, and made his way from there
    To seek a new abode.
The waitress lingered where he'd parked
    And found beneath his plate
A slip of paper, pencil-marked
    Thus—Hebrews: 13, 8.

JUNGLE TALE

A murderer, escaped from jail, to tropic jungles fled.
The hunted man, with gun in hand, advanced with wary tread.
The insects, reptiles, and the beasts pursued him day and night.
The constant vigil wore him down and tragic was his plight.

The tropic sun beat down upon that fever-laden glade.
The stifling heat rose far above a hundred in the shade.
The culprit's tongue was parched and dry. He longed for cooling breeze.
Sure death awaited one who shunned the shadows of the trees.

At last, exhausted by the heat, his final courage gone,
He sank upon that tropic sand bewildered, weak, and wan,
And as he drew his labored breath he knew he'd not survive,
But vowed no prowling jungle beast would torture him alive.

He gripped his gun to end it all upon that sun-baked sand.
He heard a sound, a stealthy move. Grave danger was at hand.
The chills ran up and down his spine. He felt the tiger's breath.
His blood ran cold. With icy stare he sneezed and froze to death.

JUNIOR

The welcome sound of childish feet
    Is heard upon the floor.
And someone seeks a luscious treat
    Behind the pantry door.
The cookie jar is in its place
    Beside the doughnut tin.
Ma leaves them handy, just in case,
    And Junior just came in.

A hurried scamper quickly ends
 Where goodies may be found.
Then out again to meet some friends
 And pass a few around.
There'll be no cookies in the jar,
 No doughnuts in the tin,
For Junior's pals from near and far
 Have just come storming in.

But Ma will fill them up again,
 As loving mothers do.
Those boys will soon be grown-up men,
 And well she knows that's true;
And so, in meditative mood,
 She craves the welcome din
That shatters peace and quietude,
 When Junior's friends come in.

JUSTIFICATION

While on my way to Jacksonville to meet a man named Brown,
A four hours' wait was scheduled in a little southern town.
And so to pass the time away I took a stroll around.
The district court was sitting, so a seat I quickly found.

The ancient judge presiding was a product of the South.
Tobacco juice was trickling from the corners of his mouth.
One case had been decided and another was at hand.
A bum of no renown was invited to the stand.

"And what's the charge?" the justice asked. "Assault," the copper said.
"He used his fist upon this guy and opened up his head.
It was about two hours ago; the doctor just got through.
Complaint was made and so I brought the rascal in to you."

"Just answer, are you guilty? Tell me now, who was to blame?"
"Ah guess Ah's guilty, Judge, all right, but you'd have done the same."
"Well, tell us all about it," said the judge. "What caused the fuss?"
"Ah'll tell ye, Judge; he said Ah was a hippopotamus."

A smile o'erspread the judge's face. He took another chew
And then inquired, "And when was that? Was that this morning too?"
"Oh, no." He had a puzzled look. "Oh, no, now let me see;
'Twas jest about four years ago, or maybe it was three."

106

"What?" said the judge. "Three years ago? You waited quite a while."
The man then wriggled 'round a bit and forced a wistful smile.
"Ah'll tell ye, Judge," he blurted out, "it happened jest this way.
Ah never seen no hippopotamus until today."

KEEN JUDGMENT

The Ark was ready for the trip, both weathertight and warm;
So Noah's clan felt quite secure against the coming storm.
But then a major task confronted Noah and his kin;
A pair of every kind of creature must be ushered in.

They wrestled with the problem till the northern light grew dim.
As Noah dozed, a vivid dream the answer brought to him.
Shem, Ham, and he would make the beast and bird and reptile guest,
While Japheth rounded up the bugs; his eyesight was the best.

So Noah snared a Pa and Ma of every living beast.
He took them in that later on their kind might be increased.
A thousand different kinds of birds were gathered in by Shem,
Each pair exchanging marriage vows before he'd rescue them.

Ham's patience nearly wilted as he sought the crawling things.
They lacked identifying traits, no crests nor manes nor wings,
But after superhuman toil upon the miry ground,
A true and loving bride and groom of every kind he found.

Now, when it came to fleas and lice and gnats and germs and ants,
Poor Japheth found to his dismay he lacked an even chance.
With grim desire to do his part he worked at topmost speed,
But seeking lovesick couples out was difficult indeed.

Though striving with profound intent, it all might be in vain.
Uniting germs he couldn't see required a nimble brain.
Few laymen have contributed so much for science's sake.
We have today a million proofs he made not one mistake.

KITTY

I had a little kitty once, whose fur was black as ink,
Except a white spot on her breast. Her nose was reddish pink.
She purred so much I called her Purr; she'd play and run with me,
Until we both were out of breath and tired as we could be.

107

I called to Purr one morning, but she didn't come around
To jump into my window. There was snow upon the ground.
The night had been extremely cold. Oh! where could kitty be?
I dressed as quickly as I could, and started out to see.
I hunted all around and called, and got no answer back,
But, down behind a wall, upon the snow I found her track.
I followed it across a field and up a wooded knoll.
And there it went directly down the cutest little hole.
I called her in my sweetest voice, then dropped upon my knees,
And said to her, "You foolish thing, to stay in there and freeze."
I put my hand within the hole, and felt her fuzzy fur,
But phew! Good gracious! What a smell! It surely wasn't Purr.

LASSIES

Oh, I've met with many lassies on my trips through every clime.
And their fascinatin' features interest me all th' time.
Were it not for all these lassies our existence, I expect,
Would be very dull and gloomy and our hopes would all be wrecked.
But they're all alike. Yes, they're all th' same.
I have seen so many lassies just alike except their name.
But on closest observation I am free to make th' claim
There's a difference if you know just how to find it.

Oh, I love to buzz th' lassies just to pass th' time away,
And they seem to like to listen to th' words I have to say,
And returnin' home I try to think th' maidens are sublime,
But on second thought I find I've simply had a pleasant time.
For they're all th' same. Yes, they're all alike,
Tho we take a lot o' pleasure while a-strollin' down th' pike.
But I find that if you're patient and are careful whom you like,
There's a difference if you know just how to find it.

So I now will prove conclusively that what I've said to you,
In relation to that difference, why every word is true.
For I met a lass a while ago, a kind I'd never seen.
She was different and I'll tell you now she really is a queen.
Oh, they're all alike but my very best,
And it's surely up to me to find a cozy little nest,
For the parson comes tomorrow to apply the acid test.
There's a difference if you know just how to find it.

LAWYER'S ADVICE

Lawyer Benjamin Bruce, an intelligent person,
Was called to defend Mr. Moses McPherson.
McPherson, it seemed, by the court's allegation,
Had too many wives for a man of his station.

McPherson admitted, though clever at wooing,
Identical triplets had caused his undoing.
Exactly alike, pretty, plump, and red-headed,
Each claimed she, alone, was the bride he had wedded.

Lawyer Benjamin Bruce, debonaire yet defiant,
Gave notice he'd secretly question his client.
Retired, they enacted an intimate huddle,
Which left Lawyer Bruce's keen mind in a muddle.

When court was resumed, as an act of decorum,
The judge had the triplets parade before 'em.
All three looked alike as to size, form, and features,
A pleasing display of adorable creatures.

The judge then inquired of McPherson severely,
"Which one is the bride whom you cherish so dearly?"
At this the three ladies who claimed to be Mrs.
Then smothered McPherson with passionate kisses.

McPherson emerged from the feminine smother
And said, "I can't recognize one from the other."
"Well, neither can I," said the judge with conviction.
"The case is dismissed; truth is stranger than fiction."

As out from that courtroom they gaily departed,
Three girls and McPherson seemed very lighthearted.
Then lawyer Bruce whispered, "Those girls are fantastic,
But haste to someplace where the laws are elastic."

LEICESTER GRANGE FAIR

Our harvest fair at Leicester Grange
    Comes only once a year,
But when it comes it leads them all
    In jollity and cheer.

Our grand display of garden crops
    Arranged with greatest care
Brings money prizes suitable
    To suit the millionaire.

Our famous supper boasts the best
    In vitamins and such.
We furnish super-soothing pills
    For those who eat too much.

Our auction comes at seven o'clock
    With everything on sale.
You'll have a chance to bid them in
    With bargains by the bale.

We'll have the cutest, whitest pig
    Reposing in a crate,
And someone's going to take him home;
    So don't forget the date.

Just make your preparations now
    And bring along some change.
You won't need much but just a bit
    To help the Leicester Grange.

LENIENCY

Joe shot his mother and his dad
    And made no firm denial.
Arrest resulted, and the lad
    Was promptly brought to trial.

"My boy, what put you in this plight?"
    Demanded Justice Miller.
"They wouldn't let me out at night,"
    Declared the youthful killer.

The frowning judge upon the youth
    Observed no marked repentance.
He said, "Do you admit the truth
    Before my passing sentence?"

Said Joseph, "I've transgressed the right,
    But trust your mien will soften,
And I request a sentence light,
    Because I am an orphan."

A LESSON IN GRAMMAR

In guilty tones Josephus Jones grumbled from his rocking chair,
"I really feel it in my bones our methods ain't exactly square."
Then Mrs. Jones put down her book. "Aren't is the word," she
Tartly fumed. And Mr. Jones, with troubled look, repeated
"Aren't" and then resumed.

"We've fifty thousand tucked away. It aren't just right to keep
It dead." "It isn't," countered Mrs. J. "It isn't, then," he
Sharply said. "We'd ought to help your brother, Bill." "We ought,"
His wife corrected him. "We ought and by the gods we will," said
Mr. Jones with rising vim.

"And there are others we might aid," the true grammarian averred.
"There are Wesley Weeks and Susan Wade, whose homes are to be sold,
I've heard. And Aunt Lucille and Uncle Clem. How they survive,
God only knows. The bank won't do a thing for them and even
Threatens to foreclose."

Then Mr. Jones said, "I agree that every word you say is so. Of
Course you talk much better'n me, but I'm the guy who makes the
Dough, and just because I didn't click when other kids their
Lessons larnt, I wish you wouldn't buck and kick whenever I say,
'Ain't' for 'aren't.'

"And all them other words I use come natural as heck to me. I'm
Sick of nagging and refuse to listen when you disagree. I'll
Furnish coin to help them out before they have to take a walk,
But you must shut your trap about the way I look and act and talk."

Now Mrs. Jones was strictly hep that Mr. Jones had made it clear.
She knew she'd have to keep in step to prance along with hubby dear,
And so she said, "My darling boy, I'm inconsiderately dense. If
Rustic slang will bring you joy, of course I shouldn't take offense.

"And now let's not procrastinate in rendering preferential aid.
We'll interview the magistrate before foreclosure plans are laid."
"I s'pose you mean," said Mr. J., "there ain't much time to cover
Ground, so we'll get busy right away and give them guys the runaround.

"We'll muffle this foreclosure gag and show them punks we're not
Asleep. I've listened to the devils brag about how slick they
Shear the sheep. We'll plank the old spondulix down and lay them
Money-grabbers out. Come on. Let's hustle into town and spread
Some honest coin about."

So Uncle Clem and Aunt Lucille today from debt are free and clear,
And certain others also feel security and lack of fear and all
Because, in manner free, the Joneses volunteered the price, and
Mr. Jones exclaims with glee, "Now ain't that purty goddam nice?"

LEST WE FORGET THE OLD DAYS

She's a-waitin' in the kitchen and I know she thinks of me,
And I feel I should be goin', for it's gettin' late, I see.
But the lights are bright and cheery and the weather looks like rain;
So I'll stay a little longer and we'll fill 'em up again.
Come, my hearty, make it snappy. Set 'em up and pass 'em round.
That's the boy. Now start the music. Fill the place with joyful sound.
Here's to millionaires and masses. Drink, my laddies, while it's free.
Lift your hands and clink the glasses to the one who waits for me.

She's a-waitin' at the window. I should be there long ago,
But the air outside is chilly and the weather looks like snow;
So we'll take another nipper and we'll sing the barroom song,
For it soon will be tomorrow and I'll ramble right along.
Keep the music goin', Jimmie. Fill the glasses; have good cheer.
Take your choice; there's plenty waitin', whiskey, brandy, wine, or beer.
Hurry, boys, 'the place is closin'. I'll be rollin' to my flat.
Here's a toast that I'm proposin'; cheerio, my maltese cat.

LETTER TO BEN

I'll give some information to a former pal and friend,
Which, in your present state of mind, you may not comprehend.
You seem to think the Southwick pond deserves no wild acclaim,
When really it has managed to achieve undying fame.

The Isaac Walton followers come in by bus and plane.
They fill our boats and crowd the shores in preference to Maine.
No longer Squam and Moosehead lakes and other lakes beyond
Attract the ardent fishermen who know of Southwick's pond.

The other day they caught so many pickerel and pout,
The pond dropped fourteen inches and we had to cut it out.
It took three days to fill it up. We doubled up the price,
Thus cutting down attendance by a method quite precise.

Our actions now are up-to-date in which the anglers join.
We have a steel container into which they drop their coin.
We never give back any change; at that we're quite adept.
There'd be no point in changing now a rule we've always kept.

The Southwick lake is gaining fame from anglers' vivid tales.
It rivals the Pacific pool in everything but whales.
We're going to get a pair of those, a female and a male,
And thus complete the cycle for producing bales of kale.

Well, Ben, the spring has come and gone and summer's on the way.
Instead of baling bales of dough, we'll soon be baling hay.
But if you chance to come around to snare a wily pout,
You'll notice on each Southwick door the latchstring hanging out.

LETTER TO RUTH (1)
(On forty-eighth wedding anniversary, 1953)

The fifteenth of March is a date we recall
As being to us most important of all,
For in Nineteen-O-Five I marched gaily with you
Down the broad center room where we both said, "I Do."

Since then many blessings have come to our lives,
And I marvel at having the sweetest of wives.
And now, darling Ruth, after forty-eight years,
We can prove that no wrench ever got in our gears.

Nine children have come to enlighten the way;
And twenty-two grandchildren, up to today,
Are certainly proof, which cannot be denied,
That we've lived, loved, and labored, in truth, side by side.

Dear Ruth, we've been busy throughout our long reign.
That we've not reached our goal is decidedly plain.
Our task from now on is to add to the score.
Here's a tip—we shall celebrate forty-eight more.

LETTER TO RUTH (2)
(1959)

My darling Ruth, you're with us still
To spread your grace o'er Maple Hill.
You've reared your brood with greatest care,
No finer family anywhere.

113

Five sons, four daughters, above par,
Without a blemish or a scar,
Revere your super-magic scheme
Unfolded like a lovely dream.

You've led a perfect Christian life,
Since you became my cherished wife.
And so, more fortunate than some,
These great rewards to you have come.

Have courage, darling, don't despair;
You're surfeited with loving care.
Although you've suffered grievous pain,
Our love will make you well again.

LETTER TO TOM
IN THE HOSPITAL

We are having lovely weather
'Way up here on Maple Hill.
We are busy every minute;
We are very seldom still.

Something doing every second,
Now it's work and now it's play.
But there's just one thing we're missing:
Little Tommy's gone away.

Just last week he had an aching
Right near where his gizzard lies;
So we thought we'd see the doctor.
Long delays are seldom wise.

Doctor asked him lots of questions,
Punched his gizzard, felt his pulse.
Said he thought an operation
Should give very good results.

So we took him down to Worcester;
To the hospital he went.
There they chopped out his appendix,
With a big sharp instrument.

Took the ether like a major;
Drew in breaths both deep and long.
And the good nurse sweetly told him,
"Blow it away if it's too strong."

114

When he came out of the ether,
He was snugly tucked in bed,
With the nurses all around him.
"He's a lovely boy," they said.

Now we're waiting, waiting, waiting,
For some fine sunshiny day
When our Tommy will be with us
In our work and in our play.

And we hope that in the future
Each appendix with us still
Will behave and not cause trouble
For the folks at Maple Hill.

LIARS

Up in Heaven where the Angels in their permanent domain are devoid
of earthly anguish, being free from care and pain, there should be no
valid reason why contentment sweet and pure could not reign supreme
forever, an eternal sinecure. But despite the Heavenly leisure and the
carefree attitude, there were moments when the Angels nursed the
melancholy mood. They were pensively pursuing their accustomed, silent
muse, when Demosthenes, the orator, a man of liberal views, proposed
the biggest liars who had crashed the Golden Gates should again display
their talents and compete against their mates, and the ladies make an
angel cake to offer as a prize to him, the most proficient in the art of
telling lies. The selection of the judges proved to be a major chore.
They could find no lawyers present; so the preachers kept the score.
The first contestant stated that his waterwheel went dry; so he milked
his cows into his pond to grind his winter rye. The butter clogged the
driving gears, which made the cheese congeal, and the whey was so
extremely thin it wouldn't turn the wheel. When the next contestant
ventured to unfold a winning tale, he decided on his masterpiece in
order to prevail: "I had a giant carrot and with trusty spade and hoe I
dug a hole beneath it and cut off the roots below. When my brother
with his tractor pulled that carrot from its bed, I was buried by the
cave-in and was given up for dead." There were others but their entries
only raised the judges' ire, till they listened to a story by a lank New
Jersey squire: "I was banishing mosquitoes on the black New Jer-
sey swale and had fired at one just overhead, a mastodonic male. As
he crashed straight down upon me, fairly knocking out my breath, I
was helpless and his feathers nearly smothered me to death." Then the
judges formed a huddle and demanded more be heard. They declared

115

that no contestant had expressed a lying word, that the yarns of such
proportions no one ever would believe, that the stories there repeated
weren't intended to deceive. Then a pious-looking Englishman decided
to partake: "I've arranged for Stalin's seat here," he declared, and took
the cake.

LIFE IN LEICESTER

When you see a rooster crowing,
    Balanced on a Leicester fence,
With his every action showing
    Jubilation most intense,
He's delivering a lecture
    Deprecating dire despair.
You may easily conjecture
    This is due to Leicester air.

When you see the members meeting
    For a session at the Grange,
If they shout a royal greeting,
    Why, you mustn't think it's strange;
They are simply demonstrating
    Love and friendship and goodwill
Are the means for mitigating
    Life's long journey up the hill.

From the living springs eternal
    Leicester's water swiftly flows,
Listed in the medic journal
    Free from germs and microbe woes.
Fortunate are we in Leicester
    That we tap no putrid stream;
Fortunate for home investor
    That pure water reigns supreme.

LIFE OF A FOX

A little fox lay hiding 'neath a fallen cedar log.
She knew the hunters soon would come; she heard their hunting dog.
She knew the tracks that she had made along the drifting snow
Would lead the dog to where she lay, so onward she must go.

116

She knew the hunters with their guns were stationed all around.
She knew that she must dodge them all while fleeing from the hound.
The barking nearer, nearer came. She mustn't linger there.
She needed all her cunning now, and sniffed the frosty air.

Then leaping like a lightning streak, she reached the bushes low,
Where not a soul could see her as she traveled through the snow.
But soon the bushes all were passed. She now must make her way
Across the open hillside, where beyond, the timber lay.

If only she could reach that wooded spot behind the hill
Without a hunter seeing her, a chance she might have still.
She gave one hurried glance around; no hunter was in sight,
Then dashed upon that open field, and ran with all her might.

But as she neared the timber growth, a motion caught her eye.
She wheeled to left; a shot rang out; the bullets passed her by.
Again she wheeled the other way and dodged another ball,
And while the hunter loaded, gained the shelter of a wall.

A few swift leaps then found her safe within the forest dense.
She paused one moment, breathing fast, with every muscle tense.
She heard that awful baying hound, then on again she flew
To where the river rushed along, and then with instinct true—

Straight out into the river cold she gave a mighty leap,
Then floated down to where the bank o'erhung the water deep.
And there she paused, her body all submerged except her nose;
She now was safe, no longer feared those unrelenting foes.

The hound came on; the track was fresh; straight down the bank it went.
But which way now—where had it gone? And vanished was the scent.
The huntsmen gathered on the bank; the hound no more gave tongue.
They swore and cursed and blamed their luck. Again they had been
    stung.

They wandered up and down the stream, but soon went far away.
The fox climbed out upon the bank and in the sunshine lay.
Toward evening in a cozy nest her little ones she found.
She nursed them all, then started out to fool another hound.

LINCOLN'S BIRTHDAY

Our nation's rise to worldly fame
    Was due to worthy men;
And some declare that Lincoln's name
    Stands first within their ken.

A man of giant brain and brawn,
  He saved our nation's life;
And from the darkness came the dawn,
  With end of civil strife.

We gather here to honor him,
  Whose life such wonders wrought;
And from those scenes in history dim,
  We're filled with noble thought.

And may the name of Lincoln stand
  In bold relief, on high
Proclaiming that our nation grand
  Shall never, never die.

LITTLE JACK HORNER

Little Jack Horner, uncommonly bright,
From his pie pulled a plum with his thumb one night,
And, as the tale goes, with a juvenile cry
In triumph declared, "What a big boy am I!"

His mother was proud of her talented heir,
Attributing same to her motherly care,
But Dad, to himself, took the credit with pride
And claimed his own quips were renowned far and wide.

Now, Jack, as all urchins are likely to do,
As age rambled onward enormously grew,
And when fifteen summers and winters had passed
Jack Horner's proportions were lofty and vast.

From grammar to high school he sluggishly slid.
He made a biology, botany bid,
But pulling the petals and boning the bug
Were not for his stature and caused him to shrug.

Imbued by desire for financial reward
He signed for a job chopping wood by the cord,
But fate hit him hard, though he didn't succumb;
He chopped off the thumb that had pulled out the plum.

Though some would have quit when the going was rough,
Jack Horner was fashioned from sturdier stuff.
He picked up his thumb, stuck it onto the stub,
Bound it up with a wire, and departed for grub.

118

His thumb knit together without much delay;
So Jack joined a circus and wandered away.
With dice and at cards he was wizardly wise,
And his wallet assumed a commendable size.

He foozled his cronies right up to the gills.
They played penny-ante with ten-dollar bills.
He rifled their jeans with a magnetized comb.
For their I.O.U. money they telegraphed home.

But Jack was impatient; he longed for big time.
He passed up the circus and started to climb.
He purchased a section of promising soil
Reputedly fertile and oozing with oil.

He drilled a deep well of the most approved kind,
And crowds flocked around to examine his find.
The well spouted oil and with criminal crust
For nine million bucks he sold out to the trust.

LIZA LOU

Ah've the slickest little gal;
    She's a regulation pal,
But her folks don't like to see me comin' round.
    Even when Ah takes a bath
    An' goes amblin' up the path,
Her old daddy comes to meet me wid his hound.
    Dat's an awful ugly brute,
    An' de old man loves to shoot,
An' for arguin' Ah never cares at all;
    So as not to make a fuss,
    Ah performs an exodus
An' postpones my inclination for a call.

    Liza Lou, Liza Lou,
You's de sweetest, neatest gal Ah ever knew.
    If your folks would on'y die,
    'Twould be nice an' you an' I
Could enjoy their cozy cottage, Liza Lou.

    Her old woman is a crab.
    All she does is gab an' gab,

119

An' her everlastin' dad is even worse.
    How my heart would jump wid glee,
    If some mornin' Ah could see
Dose exasperatin' people in a hearse.
    If they both was underground
    Where they couldn't make a sound,
We would step into that cottage on the shore.
    Ah would have to shoot the dog,
    But we'd get a cow an' hog,
An' we'd both be mighty happy evermore.

    Liza Lou, Liza Lou,
We'd have chickens an' a garden, me an' you.
    If de Lord should give us Grace,
    There'd be runnin' round de place
More dan pigs an' cows an' chickens, Liza Lou.

THE LOBSTERMAN

John Ebenezer Alpindale, of old New Bedford stock,
Was ponderously fashioned and as solid as a rock.
His nose, alas, discouraged him. 'Twas hard to realize
That any man could have a nose of such abnormal size.

Now Ebenezer longed to live a life of married bliss,
But matrimonial overtures were woefully remiss.
His monstrous nose repelled the maids whom he would care to woo,
And those who deigned to take a chance were subjects for the zoo.

This lobsterman had ample wealth to lure a willing bride.
He owned a string of lobster pots, the finest on the tide,
And so a girl of forty-six, Miss Annabella Ball,
Declared on bended elbows that she'd take him, nose and all.

Now Ebenezer knew her thoughts and moved as in a trance.
He soon began to realize it was his only chance.
He tried to bring himself around to share her point of view,
But every time he took a look he'd shy away anew.

For Annabella had defects and blemishes and flaws,
Club-footed, with protruding lips and far-receding jaws.
No hair adorned her polished dome. She boasted quite a beard.
With pimples, warts, and moles galore her looks were wildly weird.

120

Said she, "I'll keep your cabin warm and tend your garden plot."
Said he, "I hope to have a son and you're too old for that."
Said she, "You'd better guess again; I'm still in maiden life."
They clinched and soon the clergyman pronounced them man and wife.

A baby boy arrived on time and Dad was all agog,
But all reports that trickled out described him like a frog.
One said his hands were lobster claws with oyster shells for nails.
Another noticed that his ears resembled drooping sails.

These stories came in endless stream and through the village spread.
Some claimed one eye was robin blue, the other crimson red.
And others ruefully observed, who went to make a call,
That, counter to all reasoning, he'd scarce a nose at all.

One day the parson made a call upon the scene of woe.
The mother held the child and crooned a ditty, soft and low.
The parson looked then turned to see a dubious-looking dad
Who forced a wan, paternal smile and mumbled, "Not too bad."

And so it is the world around, parental love and pride
Bestowed upon a firstborn babe can never be denied,
And parental love predominant since parenthood began
May yet transform this newborn to a super lobsterman.

LOOKING BACKWARD

I fear my life has been a fake,
And now my days are numbered.
They've passed while I have been awake,
But mostly while I've slumbered.

If I could live my life again,
I wouldn't sleep a second.
I'd mingle with my fellowmen
Until Saint Peter beckoned.

To sleep away the precious hours
Is futile, false, and flippy,
Like casting lovely, beauteous flowers
Upon the Mississippi.

Good resolutions shape our fate
And just rewards await us.
Unless, perchance, they came too late,
And that's my present status.

121

MAID AND MAN

While driving up a country lane
I overtook a charming Jane
With a bright red skirt and coat to match.
Quite a thrill for a hotspark bach.

I set the brakes. The car stood still.
Said I, "May I help you up the hill?"
Said she, "Are you sure you're not remiss
In taking a stranger in like this?"

She soon was seated by my side.
I recall but little about the ride.
My thoughts were centered upon this queen.
No fairer lass had I ever seen.

We purred along through a wooden glen.
I pondered how and where and when.
"Whither?" said I and her voice rang clear,
"It's okay with me if we stop right here."

I nestled the car 'neath leafy shade,
Resolved on winning this tempting maid.
I noticed the tapering fingertips.
No lipstick blemished those ruby lips.

No rouge nor powder was needed here.
Her skin was velvety, pink and clear.
Her form, oh, man; no shading pines
Obscured the contour of those lines.

I sat enthralled, but none too calm,
As she pressed my hand with a petting palm,
And she said in accents sweet and low,
"Oh, dear, how can you be so slow?"

I crooked my arm in the proper place
Around her waist for a close embrace,
As a big black car rolled up and stopped,
And both my arm and spirits dropped.

Two men in uniform left the car.
Said one, "Keep quiet where you are!"
He made his way with mighty stride
And snatched that princess from my side.

As they glided down that leafy lane,
A wail came back from that charming Jane,
With bright red skirt and coat to match,
"They're taking me back to the booby hatch."

MANNVILLE SCHOOL

Here stands the ancient Mannville School,
The place where teacher breaks the rule
    Upon a kiddie's hand,
The place where children love to go
On sunny days, or when the snow
    Comes down to beat the band.

The place where little camps are made
Beneath the cool and welcome shade
    Of stately Mannville trees,
The place with clinkers spread around,
Where children fall upon the ground,
    And scrape their shins and knees.

The Mannville school is known to fame,
Where former generations came
    To learn their Ps and Qs,
The place where many worthwhile tricks
Were hammered into Catholics
    And Protestants and Jews.

The schoolhouse rests upon a knoll.
Before the doorway stands a pole,
    Where wave the stripes and stars.
Beneath the red and white and blue,
This little patriotic crew
    Prepare themselves for Mars.

The Zabs are there, and Sou and Fritz,
And there the teacher calmly sits,
    And dishes out the dope.
The children's drawings on the wall
Delight the visitors who call,
    And give the parents hope.

The Mannville schoolhouse parts the breeze
That down the valley, through the trees,
    Massages sweating kids.
They hear the tree toad's plaintive trill,
The blue jay and the whippoorwill,
    The frogs and katydids.

The lightning's hot and fiery tongue
Has once the Mannville schoolhouse stung.
    But still it stands intact.
Old Father Time, with heavy stride,
To seal its doom has vainly tried.
    It's neither bent nor cracked.

Bright minds have through this doorway passed,
To mingle with the world at last,
    And make their records known.
They've spread renown in every land,
As chief of bank or pirate band,
    In every clime and zone.

Long live this venerated school,
Where love with honor is the rule
    That guides the Mannville clan.

MAPLE HILL

Maple Hill! Those words of magic, like a loom our memories weave
Into visions, comic, tragic, priceless gems that we receive.
All the stunts we've perpetrated, all the things we're doing still,
Ne'er can be evaporated from our thoughts of Maple Hill.

We are living here in splendor, not the kind that riches give.
But we're free and easy spenders of the love in which we live,
For the children need that loving, as they strive to top the knoll.
It is better far than shoving, on their journey to the goal.

Tho the windowpanes are broken, in a most alarming way,
Not an angry word is spoken; darling children are at play.
All such trifles we're forgetting; bounding youth must not be curbed.
Useless 'tis forever fretting, tho one's feelings be disturbed.

We are here to do their bidding, if they ask with due respect.
And we'll find that we are skidding, if their wishes we neglect,
For the time is swiftly fleeting, when we have our girls and boys.
Soon we'll find ourselves competing, with the outside source of joys.

But we parents here are learning, that the sure, and safest way
To postpone that time of yearning, with the children we must play.
We are bound to keep together, Ma and I, and children nine.
And we use no strong arm tether; love alone can hold the line.

As the years go swiftly by us, children grow to man's estate.
Tho we're not extremely pious, we may reach the golden gate.
For as little ones grow bigger, and the big ones, bigger still,
We shall all pursue, with vigor, truth and love at Maple Hill.

As each fleeting moment passes, we shall strive to do our best,
For the precious lads and lassies, who are members of the "nest."
Maple Hill, we love and cherish, and our hearts with reverence fill;
May the memories never perish, that we gleaned from Maple Hill.

MAPLE HILL FARM

There's a spot in old New England
    Nestled snugly in the hills,
Where the dew is on the clover
    And the heart with rapture thrills,
As the sunshine in the morning
    Streaming through the maple trees
Ushers in the joy of friendship
    On the balmy Leicester breeze.

Where the swimming pool is waiting
    For a splash upon its face,
Where with balls and bats we're watching
    For a player on the base,
Where no selfish thoughts or actions
    Dominate each precious day.
There's a spot in old New England
    That will never fade away.

MAPLE SYRUP TIME (1)

The maple trees again abound
In sugar-laden sap.
We farmers of the countryside
Are now prepared to tap.
Within a tiny augur hole

We drive a metal spout.
The buckets hang upon the hooks,
And sap comes dripping out.

Our eighteen hundred buckets catch
The slow but steady flow.
We gather it in giant tanks,
By tractor, row on row.
On hastening to the sugarhouse
By divers winding ways,
The sap is quickly poured into
Evaporator trays.

A monstrous fire is lighted then
Beneath the boiling pans.
Till luscious syrup slowly flows
To gallon jugs and cans.
Then after that it's boiled again,
Which makes it thicker still.
The result is maple sugar from
Our farm at Maple Hill.

No other sweetness in the world
Can come from nature's store
To rival maple syrup, when
You've added up the score.
No sweetness in the world can be
Awarded such acclaim
As comes to maple sugar in
The feasting Halls of Fame.

MAPLE SYRUP TIME (2)

Of all the sweets spread out before us
    Upon this glorious global map,
We're sure to hear a joyful chorus
    In favor of the maple sap.
No sweetness known to man or maiden
    With purity of high degree
Can rival sap that's sugar laden,
    Which gushes from the maple tree.

The farmers, lords of all their acres,
    Renowned for honesty and push,
Rank high among the sugar-makers;
    They treasure well the sugar-bush.

126

When comes the springtime, soft and balmy,
　　Which brings the farmers joy and hope,
They join the sugar-making army
　　And tap the maples on the slope.

The farmer feels no keener pleasure,
　　Accompanied by righteous pride,
Than when the sap in ample measure
　　Comes flowing from the mountainside.
He knows his work brings joy to any
　　Who know of maple syrup's charm,
And, though his interests are many,
　　The syrup season rules the farm.

No springtime task is more exciting
　　Than gathering sap in sleet and snow.
Reminds us we should be inviting
　　Our friends and neighbors to the show.
So, hop into your trusty flivver;
　　Join the Maple Hill parade.
Our syrup aids your heart and liver;
　　Keeps your blood at tip-top grade.

MAPLE SYRUP TIME (3)

Well, the maple sap is flowing from our giant maple trees,
As our big evaporator spreads its steam upon the breeze.
Our old sugarhouse is cozy with the firebox all aglow,
As our sugar-laden tractor comes a-chugging through the snow.

All the Southwick lads and lassies, big and small and in-between,
Have been gathering the sweetness, filling up the big machine.
Now they're coming to the sap house where the sap will boil away
Into maple sugar candy, making everybody gay.

Do not take these words for granted. Come and see it, everyone.
Make a firsthand observation and discover how it's done.
Watch the steam in waving billows floating upwards toward the sky.
Smell the delicate aroma as it comes a-drifting by.

We're located here in Leicester, on the top of Maple Hill.
It's a nifty spot to visit and the sap is dripping still.
Fill your auto up with kiddies, middle-aged and elders, too,
And, no matter how you're feeling, you'll feel better P.D.Q.

127

Fill those autos full of people. Fill up every empty inch.
Take them out to Southwick's sap house. They will love it, that's a cinch.
Oh, the maple syrup season is the time we love the best.
We are Yankees, we are farmers, and we welcome every guest.

MARRIED BLISS (1)

My marriage to the sweetest girl who ever took the vow
Surpasses any act of mine from early life till now,
And after more than fifty years, I'm proud to make the claim
That when I sought my better half I used unerring aim.

No finer lady ever shared unstinted hopes and joys,
From bringing up successfully a brood of girls and boys.
No lovelier lady ever gazed through clear, maternal eyes
Upon nine sons and daughters, each a veritable prize.

No other father in the world has had a chance like mine
To gaily, daily quaff the choicest matrimonial wine.
No other father anywhere can look with greater pride
On any lovely lady, who became a blushing bride.

Well, this can't last forever. Ruth will always have her way.
When the pearly gates are opened, she will promptly have her say.
As she takes her place in glory, I have not the slightest doubt
She will tell Saint Peter plenty, if he tries to keep me out.

MARRIED BLISS (2)

A man whose name was Johnny Sands
Had married Betty Hague,
And, though she brought him gold and lands,
She was an awful plague.
For sure she was a scolding wife,
Full of caprice and whim.
He said that he was tired of life,
And she was tired of him.

Said he, "Then I will drown myself;
The river runs below."
Said she, "Oh do, you silly elf;
I wished it long ago."

Said he, "Upon the brink I'll stand,
While you run down the hill
And push me in with all your might."
Said she, "My love, I will."

"For fear that I might courage lack
And try to save my life,
Just tie my hands behind my back."
"I will," replied his wife.
She tied them fast without a blink,
And when securely done,
"Now stand," she said, "upon the brink,
And I'll prepare to run."

As down the hill his loving bride
Now ran with all her force
To push him in, he stepped aside
And she fell in, of course.
Now splashing, dashing like a fish,
"Oh, save me, Johnny Sands!"
"I can't," he cried, "though much I wish,
For you have tied my hands."

MARTHY

The days are long and tiresomelike. I wish I wasn't here.
The little dabs I have to eat, to me taste mighty queer.
I wish they'd bring me up a snack of Marthy's ham and eggs.
They took me to the hospital because I bust my legs.

I do not like the noise outside. I do not fit my bunk.
I cannot stand this ether smell. I'd rather smell a skunk.
The women flutterin' here and there with caps and gowns of white
Have mighty purty faces and their figures are all right.

But watchin' women never had much interest for me.
I'd sooner see my squirrel hound a-barkin' up a tree.
I'll bet he misses me a lot since I come into town.
He lapped my face all over when that wagon knocked me down.

But here I am all plastered up. I cannot move at all.
I'd like to hear the whippoorwill a-whistlin' on the wall.
I'm sure the thrush and mockin'bird are singin' in the vale,
And down behind the barn I know that Marthy hears a quail.

I wish that I could hear the bells a-tinklin' on the cows.
I miss the smell of mowin' hay a-heatin' in the mows.
The speckled trout are havin' fun; my rod and reel are still.
And I won't get that spotted deer I salted on the hill.

The Baldwins and the McIntosh are ripenin' on the trees.
I hope they let me out of here before the pumpkins freeze.
They say my legs will soon be strong just like they used to be.
Oh, God, be good and send me home where Marthy waits for me.

MASSACHUSETTS

'Neath myriad trees that furnish welcome shade
My native state awaits the summer night;
And later on o'er plain and towering height
The purifying winter snows are laid.
No fairer land by God was ever made
For man to wake to greet the morning light
Or gaze upon the annual autumn sight
Than here appears o'er valley, hill, and glade.

When war clouds loomed across our peaceful sky,
No state more valiantly met every test.
When grim depression's need was flung on high,
My state forthwith gave aid to the oppressed.
The Pilgrim Fathers' standard, do or die,
Still perseveres in each patriot's breast.

MEMORIAL DAY

We here have assembled to honor our heroes
Who fought the good fight that our nation might live.
We gather to show our undying devotion;
We give them our love for that's all we can give.

They valiantly fought and defended that banner,
Our emblem that waves o'er the sea and the land.
It signifies courage that kept us together
And floats on the breezes that Freedom has fanned.

Memorial Day is for us filled with sorrow
For those who have died for our country's fair name.
They sleep 'neath the dust but they're never forgotten;
We cherish their memory, honor, and fame.

We hope that the future will bring understanding
Between all the nations forever and aye,
And never again shall our men die in battle
To add to our grief on Memorial Day.

MILDNESS

He was as mild a man, and kind,
As in this world of ours you'd find.
So gentle, too, that in the night
He would not even strike a light.

When it was chill and cold about,
He would not put his candle out.
So truthful he could not, he said,
Endure to lie upon his bed.

To hang a picture here or there
Was something he could never bear,
And oft the beating of the rain
He knew must give the windowpane.

He said it often gave him some
Regret to have a weekday come,
And as the seasons passed along
He hoped they would become quite strong.

Lest it become completely broke
He would not ever crack a joke
Or drive a nail, because, he said,
" 'Twere better if the nail were led."

To break the news he'd not agree,
No matter what the news might be,
Lest he should give it needless pain
And could not make it whole again.

When from its high and lofty tower
He heard the town clock strike the hour,
He shut his eyes, so great his woe,
To think 'twould hurt the hour so.

On sunny days, though oft he tried,
He could not lock his door inside,
Because when all was bright and fair
It seemed a shame to keep it there.

131

And oft he let his lamp go out
When it was pleasant all about,
Because he felt it would be sin
If he should always keep it in.

In darkness oft he sits and sings
To keep from making light of things.
He will not build, I know it's true,
A grate fire when a small will do.

For fear that it might further rip
He would not ever crack a whip.
In baseball he dispenses woe;
He'll catch a fly, then let it go.

For fear they'd cause an awful jar
He had no bumpers on his car.
He was so chicken-hearted, that,
He wouldn't ever skin the cat.

And he spends many useful hours
In taking pistils from the flowers,
Lest from their little shoots should be
Some quite appalling tragedy.

MISS MUFFET

Charming Miss Muffet sat on a tuffet
    Admiring her maidenly charm.
Along came a sailor in Navy regalia
    And offered Miss Muffet his arm,
But coyly Miss Muffet, preparing to rough it,
    Remarked with a confident air,
"My dad is the jailer." The crestfallen sailor
    Abruptly departed from there.
But later the sailor encountered the jailer,
    Where highballs are loaded with luck.
The jailer got pickled. The sailor, quite tickled,
    Escorted him home in a truck.
Miss Muffet, excited, was promptly invited
    To sip a wee highball, or two;
The pet of the jailer then said to the sailor,
    "I can't get along without you."

So, happily wedded and battleship headed,
    They visioned a wonderful trip.
But when they came closer the Captain said, "No, Sir;
    No sweethearts allowed on this ship."
So, bursting with fury, they went to Missouri,
    And here's where their record begins.
With aid from her steady she's mothered already
    Quadruplets and triplets and twins.

The moral is plain; if the Captain is sane,
    Some rules should be firmly ignored.
In naval pursuits, for obtaining recruits,
    Just welcome the sweethearts aboard.

MISS NANCY STOKES

Ma heart am all aflutter for Miss Susan Nancy Stokes,
    De slickest gal Ah eber chanced to spy.
Wid a dimple where no dimple eber grows on common folks,
    She's de sweetest watermillion ob ma eye.
Ah meets her in de mawnin' an' Ah meets her in de night;
    Ah'd meet her in de meantime if Ah could.
Ah was thinkin' ob a weddin' when Ah held ma darlin' tight,
    An' Ah ast her would she an' she said she would.

Dere's gwine to be a weddin' soon for Nancy dear an' me,
    While de preacher ties de knot to beat de band.
In about a year or so within our cozy home you'll see
    De cutest little oil stove in de land.

Ah loves de lass an' she loves me; we both loves jest de same,
    A-strollin' in de darkness ob de moon.
An' whateber happens to us now we both will be to blame;
    Ah thinks we'll see de preacher bery soon.
An' den we'll hab a cabin home upon de ribberside
    Wid hollyhocks a-hangin' high an' low.
Wid de music from de banjo an' de boat upon de tide
    We'll be happy like de folks ob long ago.

Dere's gwine to be a weddin' soon for Nancy dear an' me,
    An' if luck should come for fifteen years or so,
As Ah sit here in de summertime wid Nancy on ma knee
    We'll hab a lot ob chickens roun' de do'.

MOLLY

Pretty Miss Molly,
Delightfully jolly,
Invited caresses and kisses.
Along came a sailor
In sailor's regalia.
Abruptly Miss Molly was Mrs.
But later the sailor
Without his regalia
Appeared less attractive for kissing,
And wise Mrs. Molly
Acknowledged her folly.
That night Mrs. Molly was missing.

THE MOSQUITO

A mosquito, pale and ancient,
As he feebly scratched his head
In a manner lacking vigor
To a young mosquito said:

"You are really very fortunate;
You're young and strong and well,
While I patiently am waiting
For the tolling of the bell.

"A handicap has followed me
Through all my years of life.
It's been nothing but a struggle
Filled with unrelenting strife.

"No such chances I've been offered
As are open now to you.
I regret it very deeply
That I'm practically through."

The young mosquito listened
To the old mosquito's woe
And declared he saw no cinches
That were lacking long ago.

Said the old mosquito mournfully
"Why, don't you understand?
I could bite the ladies only
On the face or on the hand."

MUD

By chance I was driving, one beautiful day,
    On a street that resembled a river.
It chiefly consisted of quagmiry clay
    That tended to quaver and quiver.

I slowly advanced and an auto appeared;
    So I pulled to the gutter and waited.
The man in the car wore a flowing white beard
    And a look that was far from elated.

He drew up alongside and turned off the switch,
    Then looked at his car with devotion,
And said in a voice with a tremulous pitch,
    Which clearly disclosed his emotion,

"I've driven this auto through oceans of mire
    All the way up the coast from Miami,
But this beats it all and I'd like to inquire,
    For the love of Jerusha, where am I?"

Said I, "You're in Spodunk, a wonderful town.
    They're delighted with every newcomer.
In a very few weeks all this mud settles down,
    And this road will be perfect all summer."

He started his car with a terrible din
    And remarked as the gears he was shifting,
"It's the only location I ever was in,
    Where mud has the habit of drifting."

MY BIRTHPLACE

Let come what may, I cannot feel forlorn,
When I recall the farm where I was born,
And, though my quest for fortune intervenes,

135

I'm always conscious of those boyhood scenes.
My memory takes me back to attic rooms,
To blankets with the warp from handmade looms,
With woof of finest wool from native sheep,
To featherbeds, hand-fashioned, soft and deep.

I well remember forest paths that led
Through giant trees whose branches overhead
Transformed the daylight into partial gloom,
Where plants like adderwort, alone, could bloom.
The grove of chestnut trees, all moss embossed,
Where chestnut burrs were opened by the frost,
The massive oaks that brimmed the swimming hole
Today convey contentment to my soul.

The hand-hewn rafter, brace and joist and pin
Are quaint, indeed, and admiration win
From each who views the house or barn or shed
That echoed, long ago, my boyhood tread.
The pasture bars, with pinholes in their ends
To thwart the clever cows, are still my friends.
The stone walls, each a masterpiece in art,
Have carved their gray initials on my heart.

A space of time brings changes to us all.
In spring we're young, and then comes glorious fall.
We scarcely saw the summer as it passed,
And lifetime's winter season nears at last,
And when our course has nearly reached its end,
We elders gladly meet an old-time friend:
A tree, a house, acquaintances of yore.
My friendly birthplace makes my spirits soar.

MY CAMP

I bought a camp among the hills,
    Where nature ravishly displayed
The mossy rocks and rippling rills
    Beneath the trees' fantastic shade.
To pass the night where man was not
    Had always been my fondest dream,
And when I came upon this spot
    My inward pleasure was supreme.

136

The camp I bought was second-hand,
    A woodsman's camp in times gone by.
The open fireplace, deftly planned,
    Would boil, broil, toast, roast, bake, or fry,
While hemlock boughs, spread on the cot,
    Induced sweet dreams for tired brain
When weary of Sir Walter Scott,
    Or Dickens, Thackeray or Twain.

I took my car one afternoon
    And sped through forest dark and damp.
'Twas in the jolly month of June
    And most enchanting was my camp.
I feasted eyes on stately trees
    And watched the sunset, crimson red,
And after dark lay down at ease
    Upon my longed-for hemlock bed.

I tried to sleep but forest sounds
    Of many kinds disturbed my rest.
The mournful baying of some hounds
    Made inroads on my slumber quest.
The night was warm. I itched and scratched.
    I threshed and turned a thousand times.
Each hour a million crickets hatched
    To swell the chorus with their chimes.

On breaking camp at break of day
    I broke the record from that place,
But ere I traveled far away
    I met a woodsman face to face.
I halted then, in God's domain,
    And asked of him advancing there,
"How can you sleep with vibrant strain
    From woodland bugs upon the air?"

"How come?" he asked, and I replied,
    "I slumbered in my camp of doubt.
I tossed around and nearly died
    From heat, and noises roundabout.
Those creatures hissed and sang and yawled,
    But tell me, pray, why should I itch?"
He then in woodsman parlance drawled,
    " 'Twas camp-cot cooties, lice, and sich."

MY CHILDREN

When I have ended earthly toil
And "shuffled off this mortal coil,"
No boys and girls with tousled curls
Will charm me with their prattle.
No million words I'll have to spell
For darling kids I love so well.
No music sweet from tiny feet
Shall on my eardrums rattle.

When I have drawn my final breath
And lie enshrouded deep in death,
I shall not hear the college cheer
That all my sons are giving.
My daughters' voices I shall miss,
While buried in that deep abyss.
And I shall miss each loving kiss
That came to me while living.

When I am gone beyond recall,
Deposing underneath my pall,
No grandson's palm shall press my arm,
"Please tell a itty 'tory."
No wife's caress shall I receive,
And I suppose my friends will grieve
To think that I should have to die
And join the legions hoary.

But I am still alive and well,
Rejoicing in the college yell.
I've sons galore and daughters four
With darling wife to guide them.
Oh! now they're playing hide-and-seek.
No one must either peek or speak.
But tiny elves can't hide themselves;
So I am going to hide them.

MY HOMESTEAD

There are men who yearn to be millionaires
    And others who crave renown.
And some hobnob with the Bulls and Bears
    Whenever they go downtown.

138

And there are those who would breathe a prayer
    To stimulate all mankind.
But I sit by my home on the thoroughfare
    With friendships on my mind.

My home on the thoroughfare stands trim
    With never a crack or creak;
I fraternize with my neighbor, Jim,
    Whose lips profoundly speak.
The cars glide by with their blatant blare
    Creating a fearful din.
We sit by my home on the thoroughfare
    And feel the breeze roll in.

My house on the thoroughfare is quaint,
    Which never can be denied.
It needs a modern coat of paint,
    And the clothesline hangs outside.
But I shall cling to my homestead there,
    Till the promised by-and-by,
When I'll trade my home on the thoroughfare
    For a mansion in the sky.

But I feel as I enter the Golden Gate
    With angels hovering 'round
Nostalgic thoughts will venerate
    My dear ancestral ground.
I may gaze down through the heavenly air,
    Observing my kith and kin,
And long for my house on the thoroughfare
    To feel the breeze roll in.

MY WIFE

My lucky star was shining on that brilliant, gorgeous night,
When I asked a lovely lass if my credentials were all right.
I was paralyzed with pleasure when I heard my precious say,
"I assure you, darling Nathan, your credentials are OK."

From that moment all was blissful and our plans began to merge.
There were major preparations with a no-uncertain urge.
There appeared no opposition to our well-maneuvered plot,
And on March fifteenth thereafter we together tied the knot.

139

No such girl in all creation ever graced a family name.
She's entitled to the plaudits from the sacred Hall of Fame.
Loving wife and perfect mother, she has reared her brood with care.
Not a black sheep dimmed the picture, not a zero anywhere.

Just to say that I am lucky is an understated fact.
I possessed uncanny foresight which the other fellows lacked.
No such sweetheart, wife, and mother ever graced a family shrine.
And I'm thankful God Almighty caused my lucky star to shine.

A NATIONAL SONG

As freedom's home, our nation grand,
Conceived by noble seers,
Has now become a glorious land,
A triumph of the years,
And tho it stands without a peer,
Among the powers on earth,
It has not tried to boast its pride,
Nor magnify its birth.

(Chorus)

Oh, the glorious red and white and blue,
Has stood the test of time.
Its followers are staunch and true
In every land and clime.
For well they know where'er it waves,
O'er mountain, plain, or sea,
A shield of might, the cause of right
For all humanity.

When freedom swept across our land,
Our nation's courage grew;
The glorious Stars and Stripes was fanned,
By every wind that blew.
It rode upon the tempest wild,
Or floated on the breeze,
And took its place, with ease and grace,
Upon the bounding seas.

(Chorus)

Where'er its folds are thrown on high,
Our flag for freedom stands.
The stars sublime, the straight bold stripes.
Were placed by noble hands.

140

And tho its mission is for peace,
Forever may it wave,
Through day and night, a beacon light,
Above each hero's grave.

(Chorus)

NEBER MIN' DE MOON, DEAH

Come, ma honey; let's get goin',
While de evenin' breeze am blowin'
An' de whippoorwill am practicin' his song.
Neber min' de moon ain't shinin'
On dem clouds wid silver linin';
No use waitin' foe de moon; jes' come along.
Come, ma darlin'; lets us wander
Through de forest over yonder,
For de mornin' will be comin' mighty soon.
Can't yer hear dat crow a-cawin'?
An' most likely he's a-jawin',
'Cause his sweetheart am a-waitin' for de moon.

(Chorus)

Neber min' de moon, deah,
We will on'y spoon, deah,
Wid de little lightnin' bugs a-sparkin' in de dew.
Jes' forget de moon, deah;
Ah's yer cozy coon, deah.
Stars will shine us light enough for on'y me an' you.

Come, ma honey; quit yer foolin',
Or my love will start a-coolin',
An' ye'll hab to get another honey boy.
Listen to dis lady-killer;
Come an' walk beneath de willer,
An' our hearts will be rejuberous wid joy.
Listen, now, 'cause Ah's a-walkin'.
Ain't no use to stand a-talkin'
Wid a thousand gals a-waitin' to be ast,
But to tell yer, honest, truly,
You's de gal for Mr. Dooley.
Come, ma honey; make yer min' up plenty fast.

(Chorus)

Neber min' de moon, deah;
We will on'y spoon, deah,

141

Wid de little lightnin' bugs a-sparkin' in de dew.
    Jes' forget de moon, deah;
    Ah's yer cozy coon, deah.
Stars will shine us light enough for on'y me an' you.

NEW ENGLAND FARM LIFE (1)

When the crops are housed together from the chill New England
    weather
With a thousand billion snowflakes drifting high upon the roads,
When the northern hills are icy and the atmosphere is spicy
And the verdant leaves have vanished from their summertime abodes—

When the wily bullfrogs cuddle in the bottom of the puddle,
Down below the frigid frostline of the northern countryside,
When wild ducks and geese, fainthearted, have for southern climes
    departed
To enjoy the tepid sunshine on some semi-tropic tide—

When the horses, cows, and heifers boldly face sub-zero zephyrs
In their quest for running water from some pure, secluded spring
Down amongst the frozen rushes where it valorously gushes
As a challenge to old winter with his devastating sting—

When our rich, substantial neighbors cease their varied northern labors
And depart with expedition from the cradle of their birth
To a section warm and sunny where they dissipate their money
On the dog and pony races and distributors of mirth—

THAT is when we left-behinders paint the harrows, plows, and binders,
Fasten on the double windows to exclude the frosty air;
THAT is when we do our trapping. THAT'S the time for maple tapping,
Thus supplying maple syrup for the farmer's bill of fare—

THAT is when, with muscles limber, we saw up the season's timber,
Fill the woodshed to the rafters with the summer's wood supply;
THAT is when we do our planning for the coming season's canning,
To be ready for the harvest which will start in late July.

THAT is when we, hale and hearty, throw a gay, old-fashioned party,
Crack the butternuts and walnuts and partake of applejack;
THAT is when the sleigh bells tinkle as the stars above us twinkle
And the girls and fellows snuggle on the journey coming back—

THAT is when our pastor needs us as he reverently leads us,
Though the poet's hallowed snowdrifts make Tin Lizzie lunge and lurch;
And with weather foul or pleasant, every Sunday we are present
With our old New England pastor in our old New England church.

NEW ENGLAND FARM LIFE (2)

When the morning sun is showing
 Through the vapors in the east,
And the roosters start their crowing
 To awaken man and beast,
That's the time for which we're waiting,
 When the beauty and the charm
Start our blood a-circulating
 On our old New England farm.

With the chores and breakfast over,
 Then we rise to stretch our legs.
We have fed the cattle clover,
 While our feast is ham and eggs.
Then we step into the stirrup
 For the sugarhouse foray,
Where the luscious maple syrup
 Into sugar boils away.

Here is where the kiddies flourish
 Both in bodies and in minds.
They assist to grow and nourish
 Tiny plants of many kinds.
Then the skiing and the skating
 And a thousand other joys
Truly make life animating
 For our precious girls and boys.

Oh, the farmer's life delights us
 In about a million ways.
Though some winter storms may smite us
 We have naught but sincere praise,
For no communist is braying,
 And no anarchist is near.
Here dear mother does our praying
 With a reverence sincere.

NEW YEAR'S EVE

Good-bye, Old Year! Good-bye! Good-bye!
We can't say *au revoir!*
Because, of course, tonight you die
Per universal law.

143

But ere you make your final bow
And finish out your role,
I wish to take a moment now,
Your virtues to extol.

You've surely been a friend sincere
To most of us on earth.
And tho at times you've brought us fear,
You've made it up in mirth.
We can't expect to banish care,
Nor all the glooms destroy.
Old Year, you've given us our share
Of happiness and joy.

But now, dear friend, your waning power
To you is no disgrace.
As New Year, at the midnight hour,
Will step into your place.
So you, Old Year, please pass without.
New Year, please come inside.
We trust your heart is true and stout,
As you our fortunes guide.

NIAGARA

(Since the rock slide)

NIAGARA, our cataract supreme,
We gaze with awe upon your might and power.
Your spray, resembling fast-escaping steam,
From Hades fires rolls upward hour by hour
And vanishes from view. The mighty roar
From out your throat of rock appalls the ear,
While thundering echoes, thrown from shore to shore,
Reveal the giant force engendered here.

Roll on, sublime Niagara; roll on.
Cease not thy proud outpouring to the sea.
This noble sight we mortals gaze upon
Shall be your gift to grand serenity.

Though time has aged your face, do not despair.
Our love grows deeper for the wrinkle there.

144

NO, IT WASN'T SPUTNIK

Our jet-powered rocket trembled on the bleak Nevada sands. The pilot stood impatient with instructions in his hands. I climbed aboard and waited on that sultry day in June, for final preparations for my journey to the moon. The pilot snugly strapped me in, with terror in my soul. I still had dubious confidence we'd reach our cherished goal. A good supply of oxygen and food was stored inside. We hoped 'twould be sufficient for our short, celestial ride.

A deep concern was visible upon each upturned face as, with a show of gallantry, my pilot took his place. With magic skill his fingers moved among the speed controls, for guaranteeing safety to a pair of anxious souls. The time was drawing nearer for the turning of the switch to start our journey to the moon, we hoped, without a hitch. Goose pimples were appearing, though the mercury was high. My vision blurred a trifle as it wandered toward the sky.

"Stand back!" That sharp command rang out upon the desert air. I knew the time had come when we would sail away from there. The perspiration trickled down. I felt extremely wet. I realized too late, I wished I'd never seen a jet. And now the switch was firmly turned to bring full power to play. A sudden hiss, a lightning flash, and we were on our way. I gazed below, a million sparks were streaming out behind. The figure, forty thousand miles, was flashed upon my mind.

The rocket's speed diminished. We were surely slowing down. My pilot's face no longer calm, it wore a troubled frown. He monkeyed with the levers and the throttle and the jet. Regardless of his cleverness, our speed was slower yet. With only space to push against, the jets had no effect. We simply coasted aimlessly; our lunar hopes were wrecked. Just then a flock of flying saucers closed in, fore and aft. We dodged them all but one which proved disastrous to our craft.

That saucer struck us squarely with a loud, celestial roar. I tried to duck and found myself out flat upon the floor. My clouded brain responded as I heard my good wife say, "Get into bed; that lightning flash was half-a-mile away." My brain again is normal with no stratosphere desires. I've even quit communion with all demagogues and liars. No more I'll strain my intellect to keep celestial date. I'll strictly stick to farming in old Massachusetts state.

145

NOAH AND HIS ARK

Mr. Noah wiped his glasses, made some simple magic passes,
And escorted all the creatures to their quarters in the Ark.
He was not adept in shipping and to keep his Ark from tipping
All his higher mathematics were required to load his barque.
With the elephant's admission none except a mathematician
Could compute an equal weightiness of mastodons and mice,
But at last the wizard Noah added up a perfect score,
And the Ark began its journey with a balance quite precise.
Noah found to his vexation certain flaws in sanitation,
Which required consideration quite professional in scope.
With a system quite alluring and in portions reassuring
Noah concentrated deeply with a large degree of hope.
But his well-laid plans misfired—too much labor was required;
So he junked the proposition with a few selected words,
Which had forcefulness and feeling and were echoed from the ceiling,
Bringing terror and confusion to his captive beasts and birds.
Mrs. Noah was disgusted that her husband's scheme had busted,
But her intuition told her that the time was drawing near
When the rain would cease descending, thusly bringing to an ending
All their recent tribulations, and the sunshine would appear.
Skipper Noah had more trials, chief of which were firm denials
On the part of many creatures who declined to relish fish.
Though he substituted chowder, protestations grew the louder,
But with fish alone in plenty they were served the same old dish.
But to waken gastric wishes in an elephant for fishes
Was a task that even Noah was unable to perform.
Such as zebras, goats, and asses craved the verdant leaves and grasses,
And poor Noah prayed devoutly for the ending of the storm.
All those days brought only sorrow with forebodings for the morrow,
And with fishes for a diet every morning, noon, and night,
Total mutiny was nearing as a tiny misty clearing
In the sky grew ever wider and a star shone clear and bright.
As they waited for the dawning of a welcome, cloudless morning,
Disembarking preparations were expectantly begun.
To a mountaintop they speeded where the waters had receded,
And the gangplank hit the gravel at the rising of the sun.
Then the valiant skipper, Noah, opened wide the bulkhead door,
Knelt in prayerful exultation for his salvaging success.
As the beasts and birds departed, cleaning out the Ark was started;
As the pile grew wider, higher, Noah muttered, "What a mess."
As the creatures nimbly scurried for the jungles, Noah hurried
To prepare the Ark for sailing and he promptly sailed away.

146

But he showed himself a quitter, leaving so much trash and litter,
And spontaneous combustion started up without delay.
That's the start that somewhat later caused a huge volcanic crater
That emitted noxious odors from its sunken seething vat,
And the later generations have observed these conflagrations,
As the fumes and smoke came flowing from the peak of Ararat.

NOW

We may think about the future
And the wondrous things it holds;
We may reason
What tomorrow may endow;
But we shouldn't throw away,
As the march of time unfolds,
The glorious opportunity of NOW.

OLD PHOTOGRAPH

My heart was broke with pleasure when that photograph arrived.
One steady look and many reminiscences revived;
But one thing which I recognized which nearly laid me flat,
I positively can't recall just when I looked like that.

With folded arms I stand erect, majestic as a Czar.
That lovely smile on mother's face became our guiding star;
And Sara's there and Billy Church, with all his kith and kin.
Old Maple Hill was quite a place to rope the lassies in.

Just gazing at that picture sends my memories astir,
As I recall on moonlight nights how beautiful they were.
No lovelier bunch of lassies ever breathed the fragrant breeze
Than those who got the habit underneath our maple trees.

Although I've passed the eighty mark, my blood runs red and warm.
The years have never dimmed my love for female face and form;
And if I live a thousand years I'll not forget the thrill
Which came to me from all the girls at dear old Maple Hill.

147

OLD SIMON

Our old friend Simon Littledoo has surely, up to date,
    Been anything but prosperous and wise.
He has always done his planting just about a month too late
    And has therefore always failed to win a prize.

While all his friends and neighbors were a-putting in the seeds,
    "Old Simon" would be hunting up his tools
That had been in peace reposing 'neath a mass of grass and weeds
    That had flourished since he last unhitched the mules.

And always when the time had come to gather in the hay,
    "Old Simon" would be cultivating corn.
But when the cultivating job was finally OK,
    His hay had all dried up and looked forlorn.

And when the autumn came along and harvest time was near,
    With his neighbor's produce safely stored away,
The frost would always come in time to make his crops appear
    As tho they were awaiting Judgment Day.

Last winter when the blustering winds howled 'round "Old Simon's"
    shack,
    And the woodshed was as empty as a drum,
He paddled through the drifting snow and nearly broke his back,
    Chopping green wood, with his fingers cold and numb.

But soon the springtime came again and "Daylight Savings Time"
    Was placed upon the statutes for a year.
The City people all rejoiced and thought it was sublime,
    But the farmers didn't take it with a cheer.

But Simon figured out like this: If changing clocks an hour
    Would save just that much daylight every day,
Why wouldn't it be twice as good to use a bit more power,
    And shove 'em 'round again, without delay?

And so that night he took the clock within his calloused hand,
    Clicked off two hours, then hung it on the wall.
He told his wife if all the kids would work to beat the band,
    He could catch up with his neighbors late next fall.

OUR ANCESTOR

A monkey noticed Livingstone
    Approaching from the west.
He whispered to a monkey friend,
    "I see we have a guest."

The other answered, "So we have,
    But why is he so pale?
I'm his great-great-great-great-great grandpa,
    And it seems he's lost his tail."

OUR BABY

One day a little baby came
To make his home with us.
At first he didn't want to stay,
But made an awful fuss.
He wrinkled up his little face,
And puckered up his nose,
And made a funny little noise;
The best he could, I s'pose.

He didn't have a single tooth.
He couldn't chew or bite.
But mama'd take him in with her,
Quite often, day and night.
And after that he'd slumber
In his little bassinet,
And mama'd call him "honey bunch"
And "precious little pet."

But baby soon was two years old,
And cunning as could be.
He'd walk and run around the house,
And really play with me.
We used to have such lovely times;
He'd do just what I'd say,
And didn't make a fuss at all,
About what we should play.

But now he's four years old, and I
Can't manage him at all,
And when I'd like to play a game,
He wants to roll a ball,
Or do some other crazy thing,
That I don't want to do.
Oh, gee! I wish he wasn't four,
But always stayed at two.

OUR CHESTNUT TREE

A chestnut seed sent up a sprout.
The tree grew straight and tall,
Outstripping others roundabout,
The King among them all.
The giant trunk, each massive limb,
Would yearly thrive and grow
Throughout those ages dark and dim,
For that was long ago.
Alone today the monarch stands;
Its sap no longer flows.
The lightning's stinging, fiery hands
Have dealt their deadly blows.
By ice encased, each towering arm
Has sunk beneath the strain.
Its former grace and leafy charm
Will ne'er come back again.
Time was when bears around it played
And wolves their battles fought.
Time was when Red Skins 'neath its shade
Their brave young warriors taught.
Time was when eagles built their nest
Upon its stately head,
But now the owl and coon infest
Its hollow limbs instead.
The giant chestnut tree has died,
But still it stands upright.
Its rigid fibers still abide,
Despite the tempest's might.
It stands in glory, unafraid,
A monument sublime.

OUR CHILDREN

We're so thankful we're the parents of our precious girls and boys;
Such a blessing is the greatest in the world.
How we love to watch them frolic with their dollies and their toys,
And at night to see them in their beddies curled.

How we love to see their tousled heads upon the pillows white
And to watch their little motions as they dream
Of a great big golden eagle, or an airplane on its flight,
Or a grizzly bear a-wading in the stream.

And at breakfast in the morning, all the dreams are quickly told;
Each one thinks *his* dream more vivid than the rest.
But the dreams are soon forgotten, as the members of the fold
Dash away to find real robins in a nest.

Oh, how wonderful it really is to have these children dear
Rushing in to tell their troubles and their joys;
Our work is all arranged for us, the while we linger here,
Giving counsel to these priceless girls and boys.

OUR FAMILY

In nineteen-five on March fifteen,
Together with my darling queen,
With visions of the coming stork,
We made the journey to New York.

That stork, fulfilling future dates,
The liveliest bird in seven states,
Delivered eight delightful dears,
Distributed throughout the years.

A tiny bundle then he found.
He picked it up and brought it 'round.
That bundle from another nest
Was just as welcome as the rest.

Nine lovely children, what a thrill,
Then graced our home at Maple Hill.
Grandchildren came at merry rate,
Until we soon had twenty-eight.

And we can see the welcome sign
That we shall soon have twenty-nine.
We surely have not lived in vain
And fondly gaze down memory lane.

OUR FARM IN THE HILLS

When the rising sun comes creeping o'er the valleys toward the east,
And the frogs have quit their peeping, and the night-time sounds have
   ceased,
When we hear the cattle lowing for their green alfalfa feed,
And the roosters start their crowing, as their nature has decreed,
I arise with wife and kiddies, all refreshed from peaceful sleep,
To the task of feeding biddies, horses, cattle, pigs, and sheep,
And in fair or stormy weather, each receives a joyous thrill,
For we all do things together at the farm upon the hill.

We've a daughter who's in college. We have sons in college too.
They are there to gather knowledge that will steer them safely through.
We have high-school kids, and grammar-, and a tiny, tousled head.
When they're all at home, the clamor is enough to wake the dead.
But we cherish and adore 'em, for they're healthy, bright, and gay.
Tho they sometimes lack decorum, we are glad they are that way.
Healthy children can't be happy in a bandbox, neatly tied,
And example, good but snappy, is their very safest guide.

Tho our farm is elevated, lying fairly near the sky,
And our forest lots are rated as to value rather high,
We have certain open spaces where the green alfalfa grows,
And some rocky, swampy places where the rippling water flows.
We have kids of all dimensions: some are bigger, far, than I;
So we gave our close attention to the water rushing by,
And we quickly then decided that a solid dam we'd make,
And our farm is now divided by a forty-acre lake.

Then we placed some fish within it and they've grown to wondrous size.
Now we needn't wait a minute for the finny ones to rise.
In the winter we've the skating, in the summer other joys,
Pleasures keen and enervating for our darling girls and boys.
In the winter, ice we gather; many, many tons we take.
Tho the hills are nice, we'd rather spend our leisure at the lake.
All you folks with brook and valley, and a gravel bank beyond,
Do not hesitate and dally. Build a dam and have a pond.

THE OUTLOOK

Well, they say that eighty-four
Is an enviable score
In a world beset by bursting bombs and shells,
But I'll tell my many friends
That a journey never ends,
Till the last remaining tinkling of the bells.

So, my friends, do not fret;
I've not played my aces yet,
Though I readily admit it's getting late.
When I'm ready to depart,
I will get a running start,
Which will drop me just inside the Golden Gate.

When I safely land inside,
I will not be satisfied
With less comfort than I've had on Mother Earth.
If they want me to remain,
They will strive to entertain,
For I still insist upon my money's worth.

I will take an Angel's arm,
Well endowed with grace and charm,
And sashay around the diamond-studded throne.
We'll go gliding here and there
Underneath the golden glare,
For I never was content to be alone.

They can find no other way
To inveigle me to stay,
When I've had such glorious times throughout the years.
This is not an idle jest;
If they fail to meet the test,
I will throw some monkey wrenches in the gears.

So, they better watch their step,
For I still abound in pep,
And expecting entertainment with a thrill.
If I note a thought or sign
That won't coincide with mine,
I shall speedily return to Maple Hill.

THE PACIFIST SPEAKS

Mighty men are reigning,
Private lives restraining,
In unhappy countries that have cherished freedom's dreams,
Rattling shining sabers,
Terrifying neighbors
By their warlike gestures and their propaganda schemes.

Dictatorial demons,
Seemingly in tremens,
Drunk with power and ego and with voices raised on high,
Every virtue thwarting,
Counseling, exhorting
Mothers to raise children who may later fight and die.

Sun will shine tomorrow
On nations wreathed in sorrow;
Leaders blindly worship war and shun all Christian creeds.
While they stand indicted,
All should be united
Who would crush the sponsors for their ignominious deeds.

Talk of isolation,
Sheer imagination,
Span the vast Atlantic waste in six and thirty hours,
Radio and cable,
Privacy a fable,
Chance for perfect harmony amongst all Christian powers.

Let us join our forces,
Nations and resources.
Quit this vacillating farce and tell them what is what.
Stars and Stripes are steady.
Christian lands are ready.
Rescue all Democracies and never fire a shot.

To each warlike nation
Send a delegation,
Clergymen to force ecclesiastical decrees.
Show them by example
Truth and love are ample;
The Golden Rule's the only thing to bring them to their knees.

THE PANTRY

'Tis a pleasure when the children come a-tramping home from school
With their cheeks made rosy by the frosty air,
To the pantry on the run, for a cookie or a bun,
Every blessed one as hungry as a bear.
Oh! how wonderful the pantry is. And now a glass of milk,
Just to guard against starvation for a while,
Till that welcome sound they hear, "Supper's ready, children dear."
They can hear those words of magic half a mile.
At the table all assembled they can scarcely bear to wait,
While poor father sends 'round dishes by the score.
They're as hollow as a drum, and before his turn has come,
To headquarters every plate has come for more.
Oh, the pleasure of the mother, and the father's pleasure, too,
Can be measured only by the laws of love,
As they watch with fears and joys, big and little girls and boys
That have come to them for care, from God above.

PARROT

A gentle dame from Lafayette
Brought home a parrot for a pet.
I called on her at later date
And garnered what I now relate.

The parrot to her porch retired.
"And does she talk?" I then inquired.
My hostess sniffed and said, "This bird
So far has uttered just one word."

"And what's the word," I queried then,
"That issues from this parrot hen?"
My hostess hastened to my side
And then in undertones replied:

"My bird is cursed by bandy legs.
But stranger still, she lays square eggs,
And here's her nest upon this couch,
Where dolefully she mumbles, 'Ouch!' "

155

PARSNIPS

The parsnip is a solid friend.
    It sports a true nutritious blend.
It also has deep-rooted grace
    Well-fashioned in its tapering base.
It also grows in many hues,
    In purples, whites and blacks and blues.
And some are fat and some are slim,
    But every one is packed with vim.
Its prominence has gained renown
    In every city, burg, and town,
Which undeniably ensures
    Adoption by the epicures.
No other crops some farmers grow,
    And that's because they really know
The secrets of the parsnip game
    That bring them affluence and fame.
Some people joke and laugh and sneer,
    When I allude to parsnip beer,
But if they'd only take a stein
    They'd place it with the choicest wine.
A parsnip cocktail has a fizz
    That stamps it as a potent whiz.
A couple taken with your meals,
    You'll feel like any farmer feels,
When everything is going swell
    With money coming in like anything,
So fast, indeed, he needs an axe
    To whittle down his income tax.
Of all the delicate viands that
    People praise in many lands
The parsnip to the record clings.
    It's really king of all the kings.
It makes me feel extremely sad
    To know some kiddie's loving dad
Should stoop so low and strain his voice
    To say the parsnip's not his choice.
In fact, I cannot understand
    How parsnips, either fresh or canned,
Can fail to promptly steal the show
    And make the gastric juices flow.

They have a flavor all their own;
  In lusciousness they stand alone.
No other root has such appeal
  For balancing a modern meal.
In nourishing the human race
  The parsnip takes its solemn place,
And those who scoff and say it's vile
  Had better ponder for a while.
For vitamins in ample store
  Come oozing from the parsnip's core,
With vast amounts of niacin
  Secreted in the parsnip's skin.
Though not the same with other crops,
  There's nourishment in parsnip tops.
And parsnip cider, boy, oh, boy,
  Is supercharged with bliss and joy.
Though some might reckon it as trash,
  If you've not tasted parsnip hash
With just a dash of powdered beet,
  You've missed an epicurean treat.
These statements may be rather strong,
  But they are true, unless I'm wrong,
And I should reckon it a loss
  By passing up my parsnip sauce.
But whether boiled or fried or stewed,
  And wearing skins or in the nude,
The parsnip lubricates our gears
  To last, at least, a thousand years.

THE PASSING BLACKSMITH

Beneath the spreading whiffletree from rafter hung on high,
The blacksmith twirls his padlock key and sighs a bitter sigh.
His coal remains within the hod. His forge emits no blaze.
With visions of his former wad he dreams of bygone days.
The automobile, cuss the luck, has slammed him on the beak.
He hasn't cashed a single buck for mighty near a week.
His horse-less pals and mule-less friends go chugging swiftly by,
And disappear around the bends with driving gears in high.

The blacksmith's days have gone to pot. No more he'll make us wail,
By fitting on the horseshoes hot at fifty cents a nail.
No more the spokes he'll place anew, within our twisted wheel,
And take our last remaining sou to finish up the deal.
The blacksmith's days have flown afar. His job is on the blink.
He has his iron bar alone at which to get a drink.
The Volstead Act has cut him short on many brands of booze.
If now, perchance, he buys a quart, he hasn't much to choose.

The blacksmith's days are dull and drear. The trade goes rolling by.
They simply shift to higher gear and leave him there to die.
He smokes his corn-cob as of yore, and loves that puffing wheeze,
While oftentimes a dismal snore is broadcast on the breeze.
But now and then his weary brain awakens with a crash.
A limousine from distant Maine, he smells the fragrant cash.
He gives a jarring, jouncing jolt unto those touring gents.
Four bucks he charges for a bolt that costs him fifteen cents.

Time was when blacksmiths wore a smile, for busy were they then.
They plied the hammer, rasp, and file to ease the needs of men.
E'en now the smith between his nods produces wondrous feats,
By fashioning from boards and rods, compartments 'neath the seats.
The poor old blacksmith's days are gone, unless with vision keen,
He casts aside the weary yawn and sells the gasoline
And auto tires and oils and trash to those who have the kale,
And thus envelops deep in cash his former mournful wail.

PATERNALISM

Dear Tim,

Yer raycent letter came today an' Ma an' Oi were glad, t' know that afther all th' years we've now a college lad. We hope ye'll enther all th' shports an' raise th' fam'ly name. Yer football legs an' pitchin' arm should lead ye on t' fame.

Be careful how ye shpend th' cash. It's rayther hard t' get. T' start ye on yer upward way we sold th' radio set, but all th' sacrifice we make will be a pleasant dhream, if only ye can come across an' make th' college team.

Now, here's a bit o' good advice. Jist leave th' gurrls alone. They can't be thrusted now at all, for they've much bolder grown, an' tho their dhresses show their shape an' are much shorter hung, ye nothin' see that wasn't there whin Ma an' Oi were young.

Th' vaccination mark they moved t' show their arrms t' men,
an' marrk me worrd, another year they'll move thim wance again.
Now, here's a tip from dear auld Dad. Don't ask th' raisin why.
In lookin' at th' gurrls today ye need th' naked eye.

Yer Ma an' Oi sind love,
Dad

P.S. Kape yer fate warrm an' yer head cool an' th' rest o' ye will
be in between. Dad.

PATIENCE

Old Jake had a farm and three sons to assist him,
    Josephus, Adolphus, and Bill.
Jake suddenly died and the boys claimed they missed him
    But eagerly searched for a will.

They rummaged the place but no will was apparent,
    Which started an argument spree.
The two older boys were decidedly arrant;
    Small wonder they couldn't agree.

Adolphus was rough but Josephus was rougher,
    And Bill sneaked away in alarm.
Josephus moved in and grew rougher and tougher
    And ordered the boys from the farm.

He farmed it awhile but at last came the answer
    Admitting no question of doubt.
Josephus fell ill with what proved to be cancer,
    Which speedily ushered him out.

Inheritance rights to Adolphus descended.
    Poor Bill once again played the dunce.
Adolphus dropped dead, so his tenure was ended,
    And Bill took possession at once.

The moral is neither important nor clever;
    So take it for what it is worth.
When arrogant relatives vanish forever,
    The meek shall inherit the earth.

PAXTON NAVY YARD

In all the navies now afloat that bear an honored name, there's not a single fighting boat of old *Brick Steamer's* fame. That famous warship, battle-scarred in many a naval fray, still graces Paxton Navy Yard on Asnebumskit Bay.

That vessel of the oaken frame ne'er shunned the billow's beck, and many men now known to fame have trod that warship's deck; and now, to all you doubting cranks, just please remember this, the Paxton navy far outranks the navy of the Swiss.

She rides at anchor on the swell, her colors to the breeze. All people know her record well on vast unchartered seas, while on the waters nearer home she's garnered great renown. No hostile foe on briny foam has torn her banners down.

She always answers duty's call, wherever it may be, a rescue in a local squall or on the open sea. Her guns are ready for the fray, her powder always dry, with hatches closed against the spray when waves are riding high.

No mutiny has ever marred the record of her crew, and lines from poet, seer, and bard have sung her praises true. No foreign foe has climbed aboard from any hostile fleet, and when her twelve-inch cannon roared they beat a swift retreat.

Her captain and his gallant crew forever are on guard. Let's hear three cheers and a tiger, too, for Paxton Navy Yard. Now, here's a toast to the good old ship with her paint all bright and new; here's hope that she will never dip the red and white and blue.

PERFECT DAY

The day is fine; through windows bright the sun comes streaming in.
Says dear papa in joyous tones, "What say we take a spin?"
"Hurrah," in chorus from the kids, and mother shouts, "Hurrah."
And soon they all are seated in the classy motorcar.
"I wonder where we'd better go?" is daddy's gay remark,
While pressing on the starter and adjusting feed and spark.
"I'll tell you what; let's call on Will" is mother's sweet reply,
As father backs the car around and shifts her into high.
"Not much we won't," says dear papa, "that road is on the fritz.
If that is all the sense you have we'll simply call it quits.

160

I like to drive a car all right, but not on roads like those.
To mention such a crazy thing is all a woman knows."
They sail along the county pike at forty miles an hour.
The grades are made at even speed, with much reserve of power.
"Oh, daddy, take us to a show" is Charlie's doubtful cry.
"We've started on a ride today," comes daddy's curt reply.
The trees and fences shimmer by; they now approach a curve.
"Be careful, Vaughn," says dear mamma. "Perhaps the car will swerve."
Pa turns his head and then remarks, in manner sharp and keen,
"I feel entirely competent to handle this machine."
Dear mother in the other seat seems well subdued and cowed.
In fact, she scarcely dares to breathe, especially aloud.
But while the car goes speeding on, she hears some children shout.
She can't repress the old desire to wildly scream, "Watch out!"
"I know what I am doing," snarls papa behind the wheel.
"And if and when I need advice I'll listen to your spiel.
Until that time, I'll let you know," but that is all he said.
From out of nowhere, straight across, a truck appears ahead.
The children scream and mother shrieks. They're doomed without a
   doubt.
But daddy now slams on the brakes, and daddy's heart is stout.
A might yank upon the wheel and then a sideways pitch.
He clears the truck by half an inch, and hurtles to the ditch.
Altho they've had a shaking up in body and in mind,
Pa steps again upon the gas and leaves the scene behind.
At forty per, the car speeds on through woods and countryside.
Says pa, "With backseat driving now I hope you're satisfied."
"I don't know what I've done, I'm sure" is mother's faint reply.
"You don't? You had us ditched," says pa, as down the road they fly.
Another curve lies just ahead. "Drive slowly," mother howls.
The car speeds on and telescopes a flock of farmyard fowls.
"Oh, dear! Oh, dear! You've done it now. They're lying on the ground.
Speed up! Oh, no, for there's a cop! Back up and turn around!"
Though father hears these stern commands, he doesn't turn or stop.
With slackened speed he halts the car beside the waiting cop.
"Some hens are dead back there," says pa. "Some reckless speeding guy!
I almost winged a Plymouth Rock myself while driving by."
"I got his number," says the cop, "and then I let him pass."
Pa hands him out a big cigar and steps upon the gas.
"Oh, dear! Oh, dear!" says dear mamma. "How could you do that,
   Vaughn?"
"You wanted me to fly the coop?" says daddy with a yawn.
"A poor example," argues ma, "to set before these dears,"
While pa intently forward leans and listens to the gears.

161

And now a flock of playful dogs comes romping close at hand.
They're caught by mother's watchful eye; she yells to beat the band.
"Slow up! Slow up!" But father grins a super-devilish grin,
As all the dogs escape the wheels, so on again they spin.
Through village streets all thickly strewn with autos, kids, and carts,
Pa steers the car at dizzy speed that shatters fluttering hearts.
"Oh, do be careful," Ma exhorts her somewhat lesser half.
But father dodging here and there emits a raucous laugh.
'Tis said, there's no such thing as luck, but father proves that false.
He forces each pedestrian to hop and skip and waltz.
With honking horn he clears the way; policemen look aghast.
And mother heaves a joyful sigh; they're through the town at last.
On down the open thoroughfare at fifty per they glide.
A hiss! A bang! A tire blows out. They sway from side to side.
But father's arms are strong as steel, and likewise are his legs.
The brakes are set, and from a bush appear two husky yeggs.
"Hop out! Hands up!" Two gleaming guns are pointed father's way.
Dad clambers out with hands aloft; it's useless to delay.
Now in they close, ma nearly faints, his watch and roll they pinch,
And fumble 'round to find some more. This really is a cinch.
Those arms of pa's are made of steel; those hands are hunks of lead:
From far aloft, with lightning speed, they strike each burglar's head.
The guns discharge, but do no harm; both yeggs are nearly out.
A crashing blow upon each jaw removes the slightest doubt.
Pa picks the guns from off the road, and takes his watch and wad.
And while he fumbles through their jeans, he gives mamma a nod.
Some shining gold and then two rolls of bills of wondrous size,
And silver change are now disclosed to pa's admiring eyes.
Pa slips beneath the auto seat the bills and gold and change,
And then, upon the running board, he sits in easy range.
A shining gun within his grasp, he lights a big cigar,
And blowing ringlets toward the sky, awaits a passing car.
But cars are few and far between. A burglar makes a move.
A sharp report, and near his head the roadway shows a groove.
"Don't shoot us," begs the burglar bold. "Don't move," says dear papa,
While down the street are welcome sounds, a fast-approaching car.
One massive hand a pistol grips, the other motions, "Stop!"
The brakes respond, and daddy says, "Send down a classy cop."
"I'll send the bunch," the guy replies, and beats it for the town.
And, sure enough, the whole patrol soon comes a-speeding down.
"Well, I'll be blowed," the captain drawls, "and how did you do that?"
"They tried to take my roll," says pa, "and so I knocked them flat.
"Here, take these guns," continues pa. "They'd make of them good use
Tomorrow morning when the dumbhead jury turns 'em loose."

"You be on hand at nine o'clock tomorrow," says the chief.
"We've tried to catch these guys before, and now we'll give 'em grief."
"All right," says pa, as off they go, "I'll do as you require."
And pa, with great alacrity, proceeds to change the tire.
A pleasant grin o'er daddy's face, in each direction spreads,
As he behind the steering wheel, whirls round and homeward heads.
His thoughts are on the burglars' cash; his love for traffic wanes.
The concrete road he leaves behind and speeds through country lanes.
At forty per he bowls along, o'er hummocks, rocks, and ruts.
With auto bounding fearfully, he takes the shortest cuts.
The low-hung bushes scratch the car, 'mid clouds of dust and dirt,
While kids in desperation cling to mother's well-worn skirt.
"Hold tight," says ma. They strike a rock; the skirt is rent in twain.
The auto sways from side to side. How can it stand the strain?
Yet on they go, while ma and kids lie huddled on the floor.
With throttle wide, the car leaps on, much faster than before.
A murmured prayer from mother's lips, and wailing from the kids
Are lost to daddy's ears as on the car careens and skids.
They fly through rustic villages, go madly on their way.
When all at once, around a curve, appears a load of hay.
The horses snort and yank the load, which quickly overturns.
The farmer, perched upon the top, is hurled among the ferns.
But daddy now has ample room to pass upon the right,
And, ere the farmer gains his feet, is clearly out of sight.
But now a cop appears ahead; he signals pa to wait,
But daddy pulls a little wire and lifts the number plate.
He cuts the throttle open wide, and then the muffler too;
The traffic cop can scarcely see a dusty streak of blue.
At dizzy speed, for mile on mile, through lanes and highways punk,
The laboring car goes madly on, and overturns a skunk.
Although the air was blue before, it's surely bluer now;
The fumes arise, and daddy now sideswipes a farmer's cow.
The cow careens across a wall; the running board is bent.
Pa stops to note the damage done, which magnifies the scent.
"Oh, please drive on," says dear mamma. "I cannot stand it here."
"It's better than the stuff you use," says daddy with a sneer.
The farmer's cow is also bent. Upon the wall she rests.
Pa pulls her over. Down she comes. She gazes at her guests.
She gains her feet. She snaps her tail. Her head she holds on high,
And on a hill her silhouette appears against the sky.
But now they ramble on again, with many a lusty lurch,
For papa has a date to keep that night at Baptist Church.
A deacon he's to be if his credentials are OK.
It's getting late; the bounding car leaps wildly on its way.

Poor mother and the little ones are in a huddled heap.
They bound around from side to side at every vicious leap.
The radiator starts to boil; the engine starts to skip,
As up and down and in and out around the curves they slip.
They soon emerge upon a road that now will homeward lead.
Through clouds of fast-escaping steam, they pass at slower speed.
The wheezing engine does its best; it's running now on two.
But just around a little curve, the villa comes in view.
With bated breath, they clamber out, as silent stands the car.
Within a bag, the bills and coin are placed by dear papa.
With eyes toward Heaven, ma emits a soul-relieving sob,
As daddy hustles to the church to get his deacon's job!

PETER PIPER

Peter Piper's brain was simple but he thrived at selling pickles.
He was dull at counting money so he took his pay in nickels.
Even then the short-change artists made a sucker out of Peter,
And his wife was so abusive that he scarcely dared to meet her.
When she caught him she'd upbraid him in a manner most derisive.
She had pondered separation but her plans were indecisive.
Peter'd been extremely docile ever since the day he met her.
Though she searched the township over she discovered no one better.

One fine morning Peter Piper took his pickles to a buyer.
On the way he downed three whiskeys which were super-charged with
    fire.
Through the doorway Peter staggered, saw the grocer, big and chunky,
And let loose a brand of language that would melt a cast-iron monkey.
Then the well-proportioned grocer did some very clever swinging,
And poor Peter Piper listened to the birdies sweetly singing.
One hard blow below his temple did the trick, although informal.
Something snapped and from that instant Peter Piper's brain was normal.

Peter took his pickle money which he counted with precision
And departed for his fireside with a strange but certain vision.
When he came into her presence and his waiting wife espied him,
She tuned up her vocal organs and proceeded to deride him.
Peter waited just an instant before starting in to scold her.
"From now on I'm cockalorum in this joint" is what he told her,
And his wife was so astounded that she lost her voice completely
And departed for the stairway which she bounded upward neatly.

Peter watched his wife's displeasure with a certain satisfaction
But decided very ably there was bound to be reaction,
And the lady's ultimatum, though he argued well and pleaded,
Was, that she'd not live with Peter if he knew as much as she did;
So she packed up her belongings plus the silver and the china
And with no farewell to Peter hopped aboard an ocean liner,
But it's twenty-five to one she misses Peter like the dickens,
As he plies his pickle business reinforced by raising chickens.

Now, before our Peter Piper got that blow upon his noddle,
He was mooney-eyed and morbid and his walk was just a waddle;
And he bought his seed for pickles from all sorts of crazy places,
And their bum, uneven sprouting furnished many vacant spaces.
But his troubles now are over since his brain began to function,
And with seed from standard stock his farm is known as Pickle Junction.
Since these honest firms have served him all his crops have nearly
    doubled.
But without a wife poor Peter Piper's brow is moist and troubled.

We all prophesy the lady is right now severely flustered,
Roaming 'round without her hubby for she's really smart as mustard,
And we think she'll realize the fact she courts a vast delusion
With Peter's chicks and pickles coining money in profusion.
All his neighbors have the notion Peter's telephone will jingle,
And his foolish wife will answer, "I'll again among you mingle."
She will come to the conclusion ours is tops among the nations,
And a lone grass-widow's status doesn't meet her aspirations.

PIPE SMOKING

One afternoon Sir Walter Raleigh
    Crossed the raging main.
He found Virginia rather squally
    So sailed back again.
Before he sailed he looked around;
    Tobacco met his gaze.
So he gave the tip—
    "Fill up the ship."
Since then it's been the craze.

It matters not what I may do
    To pass the time away.
On certain days I'm feeling blue
    And then, again, I'm gay.

But when I'm rash and lose my cash
    And find I'm nearly broke,
My troubles cease as my pipe of peace
    Sends up the curling smoke.

Tobacco is a wondrous weed;
    Its praises must be sung.
A man who's had it for his creed
    Has never yet been hung.
But girls and boys should pass such joys,
    Their elders all agree.
They can get their thrills without the ills
    By simply watching me.

I smoke my pipe in the morning,
    And I smoke my pipe at night.
And I smoke it in the afternoon
    To make my spirits light.
But to keep in stride with my joy and pride—
    The Queen of the Suffragettes,
I must treat the girl in the merry whirl
    To the deadly cigarettes.

THE PLOWMAN

The plowman walks behind the moving plow
And guides its course as he alone knows how.
With skillful feel he solves the greensward cleft
With pressure on the handles, right and left.

No novice can perform a task like this.
His method is by rule of hit or miss.
He'll curse the plow as in and out it goes
And blame the horses for the crooked rows.

The skillful plowman knows the secret move
That keeps his plow forever in its groove.
The horses sense at once the master hand
And stretch their harness taut without command.

"Come, Dick; come, Dan" is only a request,
But on they move to give their very best.
And often when they reach the furrow's end
They look around and whinney at their friend.

166

With confident expectancy they stand.
He comes, a lump of sugar in each hand.
The plowman strokes their glossy necks, and then,
"Come, Dick; come, Dan," and they are off again.

The shiny plowshare cuts the furrow deep,
Disturbing worms and insects in their sleep,
And many birds alight; the wriggling pests
Are swiftly borne to babies in their nests.

And while the swinging tracechains clash and clink,
The plowman has some precious time to think.
His thoughts on crops and harvest are entwined,
But darling wife is always on his mind.

A promised baby draws his heartstrings tight.
Perhaps the stork may visit them tonight.
At five o'clock the dapple and the gray
Head homeward, champing bits along the way.

Atop the knoll the homestead meets their gaze,
Emblazoned crimson by the twilight rays,
And in the open doorway stands the wife
Who holds the husband's love more dear than life.

The plowman plants and sees his crops mature.
The wife and children make the home secure.
And tiny babes, also the mellow mold,
With God's caress great consequences hold.

PLUMBERS

The old-time plumber was unique. With brawny arm and hand
He'd make a tiny washer fit against a copper band.
With magic skill he'd drive a tack to hold a pipe in place,
And then, with pleasure, view his work with smiles upon his face.
He had a shiny pocket rule reposing in a sheath.
He'd pull it out and snap it back and whistle through his teeth.
Again he'd take his trusty rule and measure through the air,
And then sit down and figure out the pipe he needed there.

The plumber called his helper, then, and told him where to cut.
The plumber was a gifted man; his helper was a mutt.
No matter what mistakes were made the helper was to blame.
No blundering in workmanship would mar the plumber's fame.

Upon his throne he calmly sat and with a steady gaze
Perused the old *Police Gazette*, and dreamed about a raise.
He needed that, because he paid so much for union dues,
And oftentimes he lacked a shave and shabby were his shoes.

The plumber always could be found around the racing tracks,
And so his mind was not concerned about the income tax.
He did not care for auction bridge and contract rated trash.
On poker, though, with deuces wild, he spent his time and cash.
He bowled a very clever game and never missed a fight.
His name, among the pugilists, was known as quite all right.
He loved to bet, and figured as an ardent baseball fan.
In fact, the world acknowledged him a first-class sporting man.

But that was several years ago. The plumber of today
Is quite a different personage, a Christian, in a way.
He takes his kids to Sunday school aboard a limousine,
Then beats it to a sylvan brook where trout are sometimes seen.
Now contract bridge is his delight. He's rather fond of chess.
He seldom flirts beyond the rules; he's house-broke, more or less.
He dallies with the demitasse, but always with his wife.
I'd say the old-time plumber led the more abundant life.

POETS

When poets sing of the verdant spring,
    With its scented, balmy air,
They forget the cost of the latest frost
    To the farmers here and there.
They can only see in the budding trees
    The part that nature plays,
But can't be hired to get stuck and mired
    In the mud of the springtime days.

They tell the world of the leaves unfurled
    To the softest springtime breeze,
But naught they say of the crow and jay,
    As they pull up the corn and peas.
It's rather queer that the spotted deer,
    And the spring where her fill was drunk,
Come in for praise while they shed no rays
    Of light on the noble skunk.

They show delight in the strength and might
      Of a rocky ledge or bluff,
But it's howling woe if they stub a toe
      On a chip of the selfsame stuff.
They sing and chant of the frugal ant,
      And the hum of the buzzing bees,
But crepe is hung if by chance they're stung
      By a bee through their B.V.D.'s.

Of love they sing. It's a night in spring.
      The lass and the lad embrace,
But they ne'er explain how some other Jane
      Next evening takes her place.
It's better thus. What a fearful fuss
      'Twould make if they told both sides;
There'd be gloom galore the whole world o'er,
      And a dearth of the blushing brides.

POLITICS

The senatorial candidate had come to make a speech.
The voters weren't united and he came to heal the breach.
He ambled up the Town Hall steps with fear his cause was doomed,
But noticed PUSH upon the door and inspiration bloomed.

He pushed. The door swung inward and he calmly stepped inside.
PUSH is a magic word, he thought. That word would be his guide.
He reasoned with a talk on PUSH he could not go astray.
He stepped upon the platform and was ready for the fray.

A muffled cheer was all he got and then he rose to speak.
He said that wars were never won by soldiers, soft and meek.
He spoke on timely topics with exuberance and snap,
But up his sleeve he kept his ace, and then he sprung the trap.

"My friends, there's just one simple word that tells the story straight;
It has the power to rule the world, to make your fortunes great.
The magic word is on that door. 'Twill help in many ways."
They squirmed around and craned their necks and PULL then met their
      gaze.

169

POLONIUS PALMER

Polonius Palmer, a well-to-do farmer,
    Possessed an enormous estate.
His income exceeded the cash that he needed
    To marry a suitable mate.

But shyness o'ertook him and courage forsook him
    Whenever he craved to be wed.
He muffed many chances at dinners and dances
    To corral a classy coed.

Erect, tall, and slender, his feelings were tender.
    He longed to be known as "Papa."
Though never a rummy, with men he was chummy
    And frequently stood at a bar.

No super-charged sodas of orthodox odors
    Delighted his palate a bit,
But tossing off bitters not fashioned for quitters
    Developed his courage and wit.

With weather at zero our hankering hero
    One night in a new limousine
Drove over to Perry's, downed six tom-and-jerrys,
    And called on the neighborhood queen.

With glamourous glances she met his advances.
    Said he, "You're the classiest yet,"
And then he grew braver and presently gave her
    A ride that she'll never forget.

His stories were witty. They sped through the city
    With many a screech and a scare.
In wide open spaces they visited places
    That she had no knowledge were there.

They danced the boondoggle and juggernaut joggle.
    He called her his Jessamine Gem.
Then homewardly speeding, the speed laws exceeding,
    Arrived at four-thirty A.M.

Next day she attested that she had invested
    In stock that would prove a success,
"He made a suggestion and asked me a question.
    It didn't take long to say, 'Yes.'"

And so, Mr. Palmer, the well-to-do farmer,
    In victory conquered defeat.
He lassoed a lassie both clever and classy
    By turning on plenty of heat.

The moral ensuing is worthwhile reviewing.
    Go after whatever you crave.
It's not to the humble the chances all tumble.
    They come to the bold and the brave.

THE POOR FARMER

It's rather hard to understand
    Why certain people think
That tillers of our farming land
    Are sadly on the blink.
They say the farmer's day is spent
    In unrelenting toil
And claim he doesn't make a cent
    By stirring up the soil.

They seem to think no profit comes
    From plowing hill and dale
And every time the sprayer hums
    It's simply costing kale.
And in their dreams they plainly sense
    The poor, old jaded wrecks,
The knock-kneed, sunburned frowsy gents
    Who get it in their necks.

It's really hard to figure out,
    With backs against the wall,
How all these farmers roundabout
    Survive the life at all.
You'd think with all their handicaps
    They'd chuck the farming job
And shave the whiskers from their maps
    And sulk and sigh and sob.

But listen now to what I say,
    And every word is true.
You'll find the hayseed farmer jay
    Will pass a strict review.

He never shirks at duty's call;
    He's game and on the square.
In benefactions great and small
    You'll always find him there.

Throughout our land the farming class
    If taken as a whole,
Can show it's able to amass
    A very nifty roll.
Their county, state, and income tax
    Have steadily increased,
And though at times it strains their backs
    They pay and grumble least.

They stage no ostentatious show,
    And crave no wild acclaim.
The thing they chiefly care to know
    Is how to play the game.
They send their sons and daughters, too,
    To colleges galore
That they may learn just what to do
    To harvest more and more.

And now, to sum the whole thing up
    And tell it as it is,
The farmer sips the brimming cup
    And what's in it is his.
He meets the entire blooming world
    And plays his cards to win.
When sympathy at him is hurled,
    He springs his well-known grin.

So do not feel extremely sad
    About the farmer's fare.
As sure as fate he's always had
    His full and festive share.
And, though he seems as green as grass
    To rich and poor alike,
You'll have to step upon the gas
    To pass him on the pike.

Perhaps right now you'd like to hear
    Just how the farmers plan
To drive around year after year
    Aboard a new sedan.

Well, here's the secret; all they need
    To guarantee success,
Is knowledge that they'll have to feed
    The world, but not by guess.

Today they shed no bitter tears
    Bemoaning cruel fate,
But keep a handy pair of shears
    To clip the coupons straight;
And so, with patriotic pride
    Plus many a clever switch,
They now may intimately glide
    Among the idle rich.

Time was when farmers up the ridge
    Were reckoned easy marks.
They'd even purchase Brooklyn Bridge
    From clever, scheming sharks.
But now a shark who tries to trim
    A farmer in his lair
Would best insure each precious limb
    Before he enters there.

The farmer ranks among the kings;
    We're fairly sure of that.
His head is used for other things
    Than holding up his hat.
And many of our greatest men
    In youth have garnered skill
By cleaning out a cattle pen
    Or slopping pigs with swill.

POWER

By standards of our own enfeebled making
    Our lives are governed by desire to rule.
Our golden chance is minimized by taking
    Instructions from some educated fool.

Equipped with barren egotistic treasures,
    We think our knowledge carries us afar,
But placed beside the GREAT CREATOR'S measures,
    How really insignificant we are!

173

PRAIRIE BALLAD

She rode across on a red roan horse
    To my ranch on the Kansas line.
Said she, with a frown, "The fence is down,
    And your cattle are mixed with mine."
Her lips were purled as she lightly whirled
    (This girl with the eyes of blue),
And then I said as she turned her head,
    "I've something to say to you."

"Blue Eyes, I'm too wise to fence your love away.
Blue Eyes, think likewise, just rein your roan beside my bay.
    We'll ride the range where the longhorns grow,
    Where the coyotes snarl as on we go,
    Where love is high when the sun sinks low;
        Blue Eyes, what say?"

She whirled her steed at cowboy speed
    And loped to my waiting side.
My spirits raised as our cattle grazed
    Together, far and wide.
And closer yet, as our glances met,
    We sat in our saddles there.
Her hand held mine, the lover's sign,
    As she said with a wistful air,

"Gray Eyes, I'm too wise to fence your love away.
Gray Eyes, yes, Gray Eyes, my roan shall stay beside your bay.
    That broken fence has brought us this.
    Our cattle roam in bovine bliss.
    And human hearts shan't go amiss.
        Gray Eyes, OK!"

PRESENCE OF MIND

One night, through the corridors, warning of fire
    In one of the downtown hotels
Brought fear to the guests, who, in scanty attire,
    Rushed out at the clanging of bells.
And all was confusion. The smoke and the flames
    Each moment became more intense,
While stronghearted gentlemen, children, and dames
    Poured forth their bewails and laments,

174

For some had been forced to abandon their all
  And flee for their lives to the street.
But now the police who had answered the call
  Would soon the emergency meet.

Among the sad guests who in terror had fled,
  One man was complacent and calm.
He spoke to a cop on the rope-line and said,
  "There was really no cause for alarm;
I simply arose as I do every day
  And dressed in no hurry at all.
I adjusted my tie in the usual way
  And quietly strode down the hall."
The cop turned his gaze from the terrible fire
  And gave the bold fellow a glance.
"That's fine," said the cop. "But I'd like to inquire,
  Why didn't you put on your pants?"

PROFESSIONAL WRESTLING

There goes the bell. The clever wrestling giants
Swing into action; 'round the ring they go.
With scowls and frowns they simulate defiance.
Apparently each fears his rugged foe.
By swinging hands the air is rent asunder,
Then suddenly the famous wrestler's grip;
A twist—one lands on top, the other under,
Which is reversed by just a clever flip.

Now rolling over, 'neath the ropes they're resting;
Another start, another bluff is seen.
That's followed by much arguing, protesting,
Until the referee steps in between.
Mid-ring, the phony contest duly rages.
They grunt and groan and pull and haul about.
They slam and whack and sham in varying stages,
Till head to head they knock each other out.

And there they lie in silent meditation,
Until the crowd has vanished out of sight.
Then, leaping to their feet with great elation,
They'll reappear in form tomorrow night.
The foolish fans refuse to be enlightened.

175

They seem to relish all the fearful din.
If anything, their interest is heightened.
Again the keen promoter packs them in.

THE PROSPECTOR

Your city is a sham,
  A humbug cluster.
I do not care a damn
  For all your bluster.
I hate bricks, tier on tier;
  I loathe your breeding,
But I must come down here
  For things I'm needing.

You speak of stocks and shares,
  Of market changes,
But none amongst you cares
  For mountain ranges
That preach more reverence
  Than any Rector.
With joy I take me hence,
  An old prospector.

Give me the mountain gorge,
  Majestic, steady,
Grub, drills, prospecting forge,
  And I am ready.
While you are aping Cain,
  With sledge and wedges,
I'll trace the yellow vein
  In gold-lode ledges.

PUMPKIN KING

Adolphus Dodge of Dooleyville is young and up to date.
    He is single, tall, and slim—
    All the girls are after him—
Grows pumpkins by the truckload and the carload and the crate,
    Fills the marketplaces right up to the brim.
    With vision, keen,
    At Halloween
    He always may be found,

176

Upon his fertile ground
With pumpkins all around,
And now and then come leaking out
The stories that are told about
The man who made a million raising pumpkins.

His pumpkin seeds are big and fat; his vines are long and thin.
Their foliage is dense,
And their blossoms are immense.
He waters them with Burgundy and applejack and gin
And charges it to pumpkinhead expense.
At county fairs
He shows his wares
And jots the orders down.
To city and to town
His pumpkins bring renown.
A limousine of latest style
Conveys in comfort, mile on mile,
The man who made a million raising pumpkins.

But Susan Blair with golden hair and form that thrills the eye,
Who ankled to the farm,
Displaying winning charm,
Now wears a ring the pumpkin king was really forced to buy,
Because Miss Blair required a soothing balm.
She shows the gem
To all the femme
And all the laddies too;
It's always on review
Displaying brilliant hue.
The wedding bells are going to ring
And Susan Blair may sadly sting
The man who made a million raising pumpkins.

But we will bet the babies come in never-ending string,
And that will be a jar
To galloping Mamma.
She'll have but little time to gaze upon the wedding ring
That came reluctantly from dear Papa,
And we all know
That kids will grow
And graduate from mugs.
They'll shake the Persian rugs
And pick the pumpkin bugs.
It may prove beneficial yet
That Susan Blair in secret met
The man who made a million raising pumpkins.

RAISING HENS

There's lately much been written of the virtue of the farm, and writers seem to magnify its vast and growing charm, the only place where all mankind can close to nature keep, and through the working hours prepare for night's unruffled sleep. They tell about the fortunes made by raising this or that: the wondrous milking mooley-cow; or porker, slick and fat; the docile sheep, whose silky wool has always ready sale, at prices that will fast increase your mounting store of "kale." The profits from the clover crop they claim your pockets fill, and say the rank alfalfa plant will make you richer still. There seems to be no limit to the crops that you may raise, to guarantee you affluence throughout your waning days. And that, of course, may be all right, for those who know the game, but everyone can't stock a farm and run it, just the same. It takes the cash to buy a tract with buildings, stock, and tools, and then you're headed for the rocks, unless you know the rules. But there is something you can do, and it's a simple task, and if you do it faithfully you'll in the sunshine bask. It's nothing more than raising hens in manner up to date. The helpful *Poultry Journal* tips will make your profits great. They'll give advice to take your pick of any healthy strain, to feed them "balanced rations," and to shun all moldy grain, to keep the litters clean and dry and water clean and wet. To have all eggs trap-nested is the sure and safest bet. It's funny how a speckled hen upon a trap-nest sits. She lays an egg, then looks beneath, and has eight kinds of fits. No egg she sees, and then decides she didn't make a score, and so she lays another egg and flutters to the floor. It doesn't take a lot of coin to start a poultry plant. It's nice to see them scratching 'round and hear their business chant. They seem to say, "Just feed us well and we'll produce the eggs." You pick a likely chicken by the appearance of her legs. A silky glow above the feet denotes a healthy frame, and if she doesn't come across you only are to blame. Each hen contains two hundred eggs each year, or thereabout; so all they need is care and feed to promptly push them out.

REAL REWARD

Four men of tottering age and mien in easy chairs reclined.
Their vision was no longer keen; their faces wrinkle lined.
While many a doubting glance was cast, they slouched a trifle lower,
And waited for the trumpet blast across the Golden Shore.

The lawyer spoke, "Throughout my life, I've banished many a flaw,
In dealing with the problems rife, administrating law,
But now, when I have reached the peak within my chosen sphere,
I hear Saint Peter softly speak. I'll journey far from here."

The doctor feebly stroked his beard and said in accents low,
"I'm loved and honored and revered wherever I may go.
I've saved the lives of serfs and kings; the mighty and the meek.
But zephyrs now, from angels' wings, I feel against my cheek."

The farmer yawned, as farmers do, and then in parlance plain
Remarked, "I'm sorry that I'm through a-growin' super grain.
I've labored hard for years to raise the choicest grade of corn,
But now, whilst I'm receivin' praise, I'm hearin' Gabriel's Horn."

The ancient preacher bowed his head and breathed a fervent prayer,
Then said, "We four shall shortly tread upon the Golden Stair.
Our work will rest; we simply break our frail terrestrial bond,
And just another footstep take to Grander Fields Beyond."

RECONVERSION

Since reconversion is the rule that we must follow now, the farmer sits upon his stool and milks his mooley-cow. He's told to make her shell out more, whatever be the cost. We'll have to have an ample store or everything is lost. The farmer gazes at his plow. It's busted up for fair. No steel will be forthcoming now to put it in repair. His spreader and his harrow teeth have all seen better days. If he can rise from underneath he'll rate unstinted praise. The labor leaders bury deep this reconversion stuff. Miami sunshine helps to keep their hands from getting rough. They do not plod along without their butter, milk, and cream. We hear no loud, compelling shout to censure their regime. Their methods are extremely slick. Their loyalty is strange. We better list the union clique upon the stock exchange, because perhaps if that were done to seal the holes and cracks, the unions might concede it's fun to pay an income tax. The millions that they gather in, I wonder where they go. It wouldn't be a White House sin to ask the ones who know. But will they do it? No such luck. They'd give a fearful roar. They'll simply shrug and pass the buck and let us suffer more. When other people congregate to launch a business scheme, at first they must incorporate and then turn on the steam, but labor unions are apart from all this fuss and flair. They turn the steam on at the start and keep the pressure there. Responsibility is nil. No law applies to them. No obligations they fulfill, a clever stratagem. A union boss, upright and just, could steer a proper course, while some we have invite disgust from every decent source. This autumn we will come to bats. I have a torrid hunch New Dealers and the Democrats will step outside for lunch, and when they finally return surcharged with drinks and eats they sorrowfully will discern Republicans in their seats.

REJECTION SLIPS

When first I started writing verse,
It must have been extremely worse,
For editors, in manner flip,
Returned each with a little slip
On which was printed words like these:
"Send in some others, if you please,
But this one, though it's good indeed,
Is not exactly what we need."

I therefore took their swell advice
And wrote some stuff I thought was nice.
I sprinkled on a little wit
In proper form to make a hit,
And then dispatched them by the peck,
While praying for at least one check.
But what developed made me blink,
Typewritten letters signed in ink.

I felt encouraged, you can bet,
That printed slips no more I'd get.
The editors were crafty guys,
And one by one were getting wise.
I sent them verses by the bale,
Which brought a letter in the mail;
And when I broke the seal in two
A gorgeous check came into view.

My troubles then I thought were o'er.
I penned the verses more and more
And sent them north, east, south, and west
To editors I thought the best.
With great prosperity in sight,
I wrote and wrote with all my might;
But like proverbial cups and lips,
I'm now again receiving slips.

RELIEF

Mrs. Winn was frail and fragile.
Trouble always seemed to come.
Though her intellect was agile,
She was physically bum.

First, her adenoids annoyed her,
And her tonsils; out they came,
And her husband then enjoyed her,
Till her teeth required the same.

Little Sadie, living near her,
Told her mother, roundabout,
That the dentist, Dr. Meara,
Pulled the woman's teeth all out.

Just last evening little Sadie
Came a-rushing from the Winns.
"Well, she's had 'em out, poor lady."
"Had out what?" "They called 'em 'twins.'"

REMORSE

I s'pose the Lord has figured out
    What really ought to be,
But ever since I lost the wife
    Life ain't the same to me.

I'd never tended to the house;
    That work she always done.
Now when I think I'm nearly through
    I find I've just begun.

I'm all beat out at inside work
    An' doin' chores too.
I'm runnin' here an' runnin' there
    With everythin' to do.

I milk a cow an' then run in
    To see if all is right.
I cannot sleep in peace no more.
    I'm wakin' half the night.

I'm sorry now I was a man
    That never cared to wait.
I know I used to scold her some
    When mealtime happened late.

It makes me awful sad to think
    The way I'd stomp an' swear
When she would powder up her nose
    An' frizzle up her hair.

It seems as if no man can stand
  So terrible a blow.
I'm thinkin' all the time
  I wish 'twas me that had to go.

I didn't think I'd ever see such
  Awful trouble come.
I don't know why she run away.
  That feller's just a bum.

RETROSPECT

That evening when my work was done I took my homeward way.
The gently falling snowflakes, thick upon my pathway lay.
At last I saw my cottage through the waning evening light.
The journey had been weary; it was a welcome sight.

But when it came in plainer view, I saw the cottage door
Was opened wide. The night was cold. Across the yard I tore.
From out that doorway, through the snow, were tracks I knew right well.
Across the yard they went. But where? 'Twas dark; I could not tell.

I went inside; the fire was out. A match I struck at last.
With lighted lantern out I went. The snow was falling fast.
The tracks, made faint by blowing snow, I followed down the lane
That led into the woods beyond. I called and called in vain.

I pondered as I sped along. Why should she go away?
No cross word ever passed my lips. Our lives had been so gay.
I kept my eyes upon those tracks through brush and wood and glen,
But surely they were fresher now, and so I called again.

Hark! What was that? A sound so faint I scarce could make it out.
I stumbled onward faster still. 'Twas she without a doubt.
 called again. The voice was near. My heart went pit-a-pat.
There, nestled 'neath a bough I found my lovely mongrel cat.

THE RETURN

I'm sitting in my office here
Surrounded by the gentler sex.
I spend my time, year after year,
In pressing buttons, signing checks,

Demanding this and ordering that
And watching all the market trends,
And I'm becoming soft and fat
But still receiving dividends.

When I was young, upon the farm,
My thews were supple as a string.
The roosters crowed a shrill alarm
At five o'clock in early spring.
While four o'clock in summer time
Was when they roused us from our snores,
And out of bed we'd nimbly climb
And hustle out to do the chores.

Those were the days, and one recalls
The carefree moments of his youth,
The ecstasy of overalls,
The jumping of an aching tooth,
The swimming hole, well-lined with frogs,
The sugarhouse for boiling sap,
The long-eared, low-voiced hunting dogs
Who drove the foxes through the gap.

A year ago while sitting here
My thoughts rolled back to former days.
I planned at once to disappear
And wander where the cattle graze.
I felt the urge to spend one day
Upon the farm where I was born,
Again to watch them making hay
And see once more the waving corn.

Without ado I left my chair
And gripped the wheel of my sedan.
I headed for the open air,
A changed, determined, hopeful man.
In course of time I reached the farm,
The spot where first I saw the dawn.
A bulldog snarled a gruff alarm.
A man approached across the lawn.

I told him, then, of my desire.
Said he, "Hop out. I'll show you 'round."
Said I, "Your aid I won't require;
I'm quite familiar with this ground.
I know each hill. I know each knoll.

I well remember old-time scenes.
I'm friendly with the swimming hole,
The level places and ravines."

So, left alone, I made my way
Across the lower orchard piece
To where the men were making hay,
And, bless me, wonders never cease,
For I recalled that hay would rot
Unless we dried it well, but now
They grind it green, and like a shot
It's blown through tubing to the mow.

I wandered to the swimming pool.
A million ducks were quartered here.
No longer exquisitely cool,
No longer infinitely clear.
My way led through tomato vines;
I picked a few and sought the shade.
I had not read the warning signs,
"Don't touch the fruit. They've just been sprayed."

I sauntered down below the shed
To where the sugarhouse reposed.
My hopes ran high but there, instead,
A thousand pigs demurely dozed.
My quest for things that I had known
Resulted in complete dismay.
As I meandered there alone
I did it in a dreamy way.

No oaken bucket at the well,
No well-sweep with its welcome groan,
But then I saw, I'm pleased to tell,
My carved initials on that stone.
More memories: a beech, a hill,
Four carved initials in a heart.
I found that tree, and lingering still
Another trace of boyhood art.

ROBIN'S TALE

In Wildwood resided an old mother robin
    With passion for home in her breast.
The tractors and autos had banished old dobbin.
    No horse hairs she found for her nest.

She knew that coarse fibers from bunchgrass and clover
    Would cause her dear fledglings remorse;
So scanning the countryside over and over
    She faithfully searched for a horse.

Now horses were scarce for the foregoing reason,
    But lady luck haply appeared.
She sponsored the fashion for bobbed hair that season,
    And ladies were skillfully sheared.

The robin discovered the tresses, discarded,
    And bore them in haste to her tree.
Again her dear babies were properly guarded,
    A tribute to fashion's decree.

Now, girls, this entreaty is herewith appended
    For those who still cling to the knob;
Lest robin's career be indelibly ended,
    Please aid by adopting the bob.

SADIE

There's the dearest little lady,
And they call her "Sunshine Sadie."
She is just eighteen and lives with Uncle Ned.
She's the sweetest little blessing,
And I saw her once undressing—
Baby brother when 'twas time he was in bed.

On the street one day last summer
She was talking to a drummer,
In a doorway where the men come strolling in,
And altho she had a ring on
She had not a blessed thing on—
From her forehead all the way down to her chin.

She was at the beach one day
Where the people romp and play.
It was wonderful to see her on the sand.
Oh! but, boys, she was a beaut,
When she removed her bathing suit—
From a satchel which she carried in her hand.

SAFETY FIRST

A union mason labored fifty feet above the ground.
The scaffolding was narrow so with care he moved around.
He had an honest helper pulling up the lime and brick.
The mason's name was Patrick and the helper's name was Dick.

Now Dickey whistled Irish tunes from early morn till night.
Melodious they were and furnished Patrick great delight—
And as he swung his trowel to the rhythm and the rhyme,
The bricks and mortar nestled in the wall in record time.

One day while Patrick labored to the "Money Musk" refrain,
With Dickey whistling double-quick, it started in to rain,
And Patrick slipped and down he went. A guy wire broke his fall,
And there he hung astride the strand. He wasn't hurt at all.

"Hould tight," said Dickey, "where ye are. Oi'll have ye safe and soun';
Oi'll shove a ladder up t' ye as soon as Oi get down."
He scaled the wall and dropped inside and downward made his way,
But when he reached the sidewalk there poor crumpled Patrick lay.

"Ah, what th' heck!" said kneeling Dick. "Yer arms and legs are broke.
Th' ladder would have done th' trick." And then poor Patrick spoke,
"Oh, shut yer mouth an' call th' van. Oi sure made no mistake;
Oi thought 'twas best to come on down; the bloomin' wire might break."

SAILOR'S DREAM

In the shadows of the fir trees where the air is moist with dew,
There's a mountain maiden waitin' for her sailor man in blue.
And I'm longin' to be with her where the tremblin' branches sway,
And it won't be long, I'm thinkin', till we're sailin' up that way.
    When our ship sails up the bay,
    I'll be goin' there to stay.
I can hear the thrush a-callin' and the bluebird and the jay.
    When our ship sails up the bay,
    I will gladly luff away
To the breeze beneath the fir trees, when our ship sails up the bay.

It's no use to try to think that I am happy way out here,
When my heart is in the mountains where the sky is bright and clear.
I have met with girls a-plenty but they're lackin' in the grace
Of the one I love so dearly, in that far-off northern place.

I am thinkin' of a face,
In that far-off northern place,
And a smile that clearly beckons for a lover's fond embrace.
In that far-off northern place,
There's a thought I can't efface
Of a most appealin' vision, in that far-off northern place.

When I see the foam a-fallin' all about this grimy deck,
And I hear the seamen cursin' at our poor, old sailin' wreck,
Then I think of mossy meadows, soft as cushions filled with air,
And the same old moon a-shinin' for my sweetheart over there.
For my sweetheart over there
With the brownish, wavy hair,
I've a feelin' for the future that's entirely our affair.
For my sweetheart over there,
No one like her anywhere,
I'd be happy just a-livin' for my sweetheart over there.

Oh, I'm sick of watchin' sea gulls come a-swoopin' through the spray,
And these strainin' sails remind me that my heart is far away.
Though these ports are overflowin' with fair maidens, love inclined,
There is nothin' here to tempt me from that girl I left behind.
To the girl I left behind
My whole future is assigned.
With this blasted voyage over, as a sailor I've resigned,
And if Providence is kind,
With her arm in mine entwined
I shall wander 'neath the fir trees with the girl I left behind.

SAILOR'S SWEETHEART

With the tropic breeze a-blowin' and the sea a little rough,
With the mainsail like a billow and the skipper on the luff,
Then I lean upon the taffrail and my heart is filled with glee,
As I glimpse a merry mermaid climbin' up the rope to me,
Climbin' up the rope to me, from that choppy, salty sea,
With her golden hair a-drippin' as she snuggles up to me;
As she nestles close to me I can plainly feel and see
That a mermaid is the sweetheart for a sailor.

With my mermaid close beside me we converse on many things,
Of the soft sea island music and the charm of wedding rings,
How another wicked sailor who would steal her heart away
Got a South Atlantic ducking as she slithered through the spray,

How she vanished through the spray from the billows in the bay
And espied my ship a-layin' in the shadows, dark and gray;
Up the side she made her way and I clearly heard her say,
    "A mermaid is the sweetheart for a sailor."

SALLY

When Sally went to boarding school
    To polish up her talents,
Her Dad's response was rather cool;
    His bankbook lost its balance.
But Mother took a different cue
    Regarding darling Sally.
She argued that a mountain view
    Surpassed one from the valley.

Now Sally was a winsome lass,
    Quite lacking in decorum.
She barely mustered marks to pass
    But had the looks galorum,
And when for college she enrolled
    Dad's smile was far from sunny,
But Mother pleaded and cajoled
    And Dad dug up the money.

But here she met the swanky set,
    The Bramans and the Bruces,
And when she craved for something wet
    She sipped imported juices,
And she and Junior Bruce were wed,
    Which gave her recognition,
And Ma to Pa in triumph said,
    "How's that for intuition?"

But then the Great Depression came.
    The Bruces met disaster.
They saved alone their precious name,
    With poverty their master.
And consequently once again
    Young Junior Bruce and Sally
Were seen aboard a cattle train
    Returning to the valley.

Pa had the latchstring hanging out,
    A sign that could be trusted.
He'd heard it whispered roundabout
    That Senior Bruce was busted.
And when they heard a gentle knock,
    Appealing for admission,
Both Pa and Mother feigned a shock,
    Just like a famed magician.

And when the truth was fully told,
    Their poverty confessing,
They welcomed them within the fold
    With true parental blessing.
Said Pa, "We have an extra room,
    A most convenient factor:
While Sally wields the household broom,
    The lad can run the tractor."

The scion of a millionaire,
    By all accounts and notions,
Is really not supposed to care
    For tractor speeds and motions,
But Junior Bruce let out no squalls;
    Next morning out he bustled.
He donned a pair of overalls,
    And how that tractor hustled!

Now Junior Bruce was far from dead.
    He made a little dingus,
And craftily to Sally said—
    "A fortune it will bring us."
He patented the tiny thing
    And Dad's mazuma paid it.
It was a novel piston ring.
    A corporation made it.

It revolutionized the trade.
    Their hopes became exalted,
And from the profits that he made
    A million bucks he salted.
And that's the time when Junior Bruce,
    And precious little Sally,
And Ma and Pa had no excuse
    For lingering in the valley.

They promptly left the ancient farm
    And to the city sallied.
Again they met the social charm
    And with the champagne dallied.
But Ma collapsed and Pat got drunk.
    A plane received their booking.
They landed on the farm kerplunk,
    And Ma resumed her cooking.

The piston rings are going strong
    For Junior Bruce and Sally,
And baby Bruces come along
    So fast it's hard to tally.
And Senior Bruce and Mamma Bruce
    Revere their son and daughter,
Who keep their purse strings hanging loose,
    Much looser than they oughter.

SANTA CLAUS

The Christmas-tide is drawing near, the usual time for joy and cheer, in city or in town. We hang each stocking in its place, beside the chimney, just in case old Santa Claus comes down. Some folks believe in Santa Claus, while others don't and just because they're doubters, one and all, but ask the girls and ask the boys about their gifts of sweets and toys, when Santa makes his call.

Let Santa Claus forever shine, for you and me, for yours and mine, to symbolize goodwill. The world is torn by life's demands. May Santa Claus to many lands pursue his journey still. The only nation on the earth that still is blest with joy and mirth, the good old U.S.A.—we certainly have righteous cause to still believe in Santa Claus upon each Christmas day.

To those who fill the air with gloom, proclaiming dear old Santa's doom, and causing many a frown, just quit your crazy yawls and yelps and join the crowd which always helps instead of tearing down. It may be foolish to complain, against a badly addled brain, whose owner may be nuts, but here's a message I'll convey: dear Santa Claus is here to stay; no ifs, no ands, no buts.

SAWMILL

Beneath the giant maple trees the Southwick sawmill stands.
Depression days no more are here, prosperity expands.
Three hundred acres constitute our old ancestral place.
We love each acre, broad and grand. We're not hemmed in for space.

The views from north, east, south, and west have always been our pride,
Since long ago I ventured forth, returning with my bride.
No beauty spot was ever planned, designed to give a thrill
To anyone at any time surpassing Maple Hill.

The Liscombs and the Martha Stripes, the favorites of us all,
Hang temptingly before our eyes until the early fall.
The tennis court where formerly we watched the racquets flash
Is now obscured and deeply strewn with sawdust, slabs, and trash.

No sawmill can enhance the charm of Nature's gold and green.
No sawmill shack or sawdust pile can beautify the scene.
I hope before I die my boys will heed a righteous cause
And clear away that cherished spot and leave it as it was.

SCRUBS

One afternoon a neighbor came to call on Mrs. Jones.
She found her washing at the tub with aches, and pains, and groans.
"How do you do?" the neighbor said. "You're surely all tired out."
"You speak the truth," said Mrs. Jones. "Of that there is no doubt.
I scrub, and scrub, and scrub, and scrub, and then I'm never done.
My hands are sore; my back is lame; I have no time for fun."
Just then the door was opened wide, and Farmer Jones came in.
He threw himself upon the couch, a figure bent and thin.
"I cannot make the old farm pay; my cows and pigs are scrubs.
I work all day, but nothing gain; that's where the harness rubs."
The neighbor spoke in measured tones. "Cut out the scrubs," she said.
"Cut out the scrubs in house and barn, and then you'll forge ahead."
"That's good advice," said Farmer Jones. "Just leave the rest to me.
I'll sell out every scrub I own and buy some pedigree."
True to his word an auction sale cleaned out his bunch of scrubs,
And all his wife's old washing-boards, and boilers, stools, and tubs.

And in their places, purebred stock came on the farm to stay.
And a wash-machine of late design appeared that very day.
Now Farmer Jones tells every friend, who plows and hoes, and grubs,
That the best advice he's ever had, is this: "Cut out the scrubs."

SENTIMENTAL SALLY

I've been travelin' far and wide in many lands,
From far northern reaches to the coral strands,
Meetin' many lassies, every shape and kind.
I could take my pick but I've a lass in mind—
Slippin' through the shadows with her arm in mine,
Slyly whisperin' secrets 'neath a friendly pine,
Thinkin' of a cottage, ivy round the door,
Where together we may live forever more.

Sweeter than the lilies in the verdant glade,
Cheeks adorned with roses that will never fade,
Ruby lips a-waitin', saucy as can be,
Sentimental Sally is the lass for me.

When the day is closin' and my work is done,
We'll be idly waitin' for the settin' sun;
Twilight beckons softly by the rollin' sea
With the only one who means the world to me—
Listenin' to the breakin' billows on the shore,
Thinkin' what we've thought so many times before,
Plannin' for the future with our hearts aflame,
Waitin' for the day when she will change her name.

Sweeter than the lilies in the verdant glade,
Cheeks adorned with roses that will never fade,
Ruby lips a-waitin', saucy as can be,
Sentimental Sally is the lass for me.

SEQUOIA

Oh, giant tree, grand monarch of your kind,
We bow to you in awe and reverence.
Your worthy mission, Heaven and earth to bind,
You've well fulfilled, and will for centuries hence.

Two thousand years ago a sprouting seed
Took root and started upward toward the blue.
The laws of nature then and there decreed
That on this day that sprout should compass you.

Three hundred feet of majesty are yours.
One hundred feet of girth you proudly claim.
No living work of God so long endures
As does the fiber in your mighty frame.

We fain would recognize, oh, giant tree,
The universe the vault, and you the key.

SLOW ACTION

I met a friend of long ago upon the street one day.
As years had vanished since we'd met, we fooled two hours away
Upon the sidewalk, talking o'er the scenes of other days,
While just across the street an open window met our gaze.

Within the room, two stalwart men, quite plainly to be seen,
Sat facing one another with about three feet between.
Their heads and shoulders only showed above the windowsill,
And as we gazed we noted they were absolutely still.

We saw that they were richly dressed and each wore a golfing cap.
They seemed to gaze unceasingly upon each other's lap.
They weren't asleep, we both avowed. Their eyes were opened wide,
But still they couldn't stiller be if there they had sat and died.

For just one hour we watched those men, immobile as concrete.
From out a doorway stepped a youth. He strolled across the street.
I asked him if he knew the guys, and he replied, "Oh, yes.
Why, that's my dad and Uncle Ebenezer playing chess."

SOLDIER'S LAMENT

In the shadow of a tower
On the isle of Okinawa
Stood a Filipino maiden coyly signaling to me,
And that signal meant a greeting
To be followed by a meeting,
But a Major saw it also from beneath a banyan tree,
Just my luck that he was standing underneath that banyan tree.

I resolved when drill was over
To meander in the clover
With that maiden who was waiting in the shadow of the tower,
When no major, tough and fierce,
Would be snooping round to see us,
As we hastened through the clover to some low, sequestered bower,
To the shadows and the silence of some Okinawa bower.

Then headquarters sent these orders—
"Take your troops across the borders,
Where the boys need reinforcements with the enemy at bay."
So we left, equipment laden,
And my Okinawa maiden,
Standing sheltered by the tower as we slowly moved away,
Gave a final, futile signal as I sadly moved away.

Thus the tragic moment ended
Sooner than we had intended,
But the orders in the army make you anything but free.
Every move is scientific,
As we sail the broad Pacific,
Far away from Okinawa nestled in the China Sea,
And the sweetest, neatest maiden who is waiting there for me.

SPEEDING

How fascinating 'tis to sit
    Behind the steering wheel
And shoot ahead until we hit
    A speed we'd fain conceal.
We like to step upon the gas
    And watch the landscape slide,
And all is well unless, alas,
    We into trouble glide.

And then we see our sad mistake,
    Although it's quite too late.
We knew we couldn't trust the brake
    At such a fearful gait,
But, hoping all would be serene,
    We let old baby bowl,
And now they're sewing up our spleen
    And vanishing our roll.

194

We often start upon our trips
    Contented and sublime.
We figure out if nothing slips
    We'll rumble in on time,
But seldom due allowance make
    For unforeseen delays,
And then our common sense forsake
    And get the speeding craze.

It's well to get an early start
    Avoiding all the rush,
And not in early life depart
    Amid the funeral hush.
Less speed and just a little care
    Will make our course exact,
And consequently we'll be there
    With all our brains intact.

Each minute is a precious thing.
    Why throw them all away?
Why haste to hear the angels sing
    A mournful roundelay?
Congestion at Saint Peter's gate
    Will surely come about,
Unless the speeding we abate
    And words of caution shout.

Let's cut the crazy speeding out,
    Relieve the public mind.
Let's cause less chance for wings to sprout
    On man and womankind.
Let's drive while using common sense,
    So none may criticize,
And thus delay our journey hence
    To mansions in the skies.

THE SPINSTER

A wealthy old maid of endurable strain
Held marriage for years with disgust and disdain,
But, suddenly, friends were surprised at the news,
She'd developed decidedly different views.

195

They held consultations with cries of alarm,
When she sold out her mansion and moved to the farm.
They were puzzled and couldn't quite figure out why
The spinster they'd known had a gleam in her eye.

With consummate skill she proceeded in haste
To stock up her acres with excellent taste.
She bought a ram for each sheep and roosters for hens,
And put them together in separate pens.
In fact, every creature of female design,
From the cat on the couch to the pedigreed swine,
Had a spouse all her own and contentment was rife,
As each male was supplied with a suitable wife.

These perfect arrangements continued awhile.
The wealthy old maid wore a satisfied smile,
But the neighbors had noticed a handsome he-man
Had been hanging around and observing the plan.
So shortly thereafter deep rumblings spread.
The news got around the old maid was to wed,
And deep speculation was bandied abroad.
Her friends and relations were audibly awed.

The wedding took place with elaborate flair.
Observers pronounced them a miracle pair,
And all seemed serene for a long wedded life
To this man of the world and his gullible wife.
Now hubby, possessing each masculine trait,
Surprised and bewildered his delicate mate.
So much so, in fact, that divorce closed the page
With that horrible man of indefinite age.

With things back to normal her plans didn't wait.
She sold every male on her farming estate.
Her terse explanation left nothing in doubt.
"The male of the species is royally out."
No words can describe the disconsolate state
Of those husbandless females deploring their fate,
And no one could doubt that the plans they had laid
Didn't jibe with the views of the former old maid.

SQUIRRELS

It was early in October. I was walking through the wood,
Where red squirrels were so wrapped in work and play.
They were gathering up the chestnuts, sorting out the bad from good,
Getting ready for a cold, bleak, winter day.

196

As they rushed around quite near me, they would chatter and complain.
I was not so very welcome, I could see.
But they'd whisk away the chestnuts, and come rushing back again,
And at last they paid no heed at all to me.

So I stood there scarcely breathing, as they gathered in their store,
And they toiled so hard their winter's food to save.
As in the shade I stood there, I was thinking o'er and o'er,
What a lesson that those little squirrels gave.

Just then I saw a figure coming noiselessly along;
'Twas a hunter, and a gun was in his hand.
"Do not shoot!" I sternly warned him, and my voice was rather strong.
"Don't you know you're trespassing on posted land?"

So he turned around and left us, all the squirrels there, and me.
And the squirrels romped and had a lot of fun.
Then they gathered on the branches of the very nearest tree,
And I think they knew exactly what I'd done.

THE STAGECOACH

The stagecoach with one passenger rolled on toward Devil's Den.
Both driver and the passenger were known as silent men.
At last the driver's spirit moved. He feebly crossed his legs,
And, turning to the passenger, inquired, "Do you like eggs?"

For mile on mile they bumped along. The road with ruts was strewn.
The day was hot and sultry as is common in mid-June.
But now the passenger within awakened more or less;
With affable tranquillity he slowly answered, "Yes."

They spent the night at Devil's Den and swapped the bags of mail.
The stagecoach started lazily upon the backward trail.
The selfsame passenger again massaged his heated brow,
And listened as the driver asked the pointed question, "How?"

Along toward night, and as they neared the tiresome journey's end,
At Carson City lying snugly hid around the bend,
With visions dull and dreamy of the ending of the ride,
The passenger rolled over on the seat and answered, "Fried."

STOCK MARKET

Josephus Jones to Mrs. Jones remarked while playing pitch, "I really
feel it in my bones we'll soon be very rich. My friends and pals are
buying stocks; if what they say is true, the currency in sheaves and

197

shocks is falling from the blue; so why should we sit calmly by and watch the others win? We're nearly old enough to die; what say we take a spin? Nine thousand dollars in the bank are drawing two percent. Let's pull it out and turn the crank and stop this paying rent."

Then Mrs. J. laid down her cards and said to Mr. J., "We've labored hard as pals and pards for many a weary day. We have our little bank account; we'll need it by and by; so let's not tap the family fount for fear it may run dry." But Farmer Jones was not convinced; he longed for fortune's fame. In chosen phrases far from minced his ultimatum came: "Tomorrow out it comes, by gosh." His nostrils spouted fire. "I've played the roll of crook-necked squash as long as I desire."

Next morning Farmer Jones arose and sought the broker's lair. Twelve hundred shares of Hollow Hose on margin was his share. He watched the tape till closing time, two thousand berries net. He felt elated and sublime and Hose was running yet. For several days the market trend went wildly on its way, but there is sure to be an end to every rainbow ray, and, though at first the drop was slight, recoveries were there, and Farmer Jones felt no affright about the Wall Street Bear.

Both Mr. J. and Mrs. J. would now be fixed for life, if he had trod the safest way and listened to his wife. She counseled him to sell at once and on the velvet stand. He argued that he'd be a dunce to chuck a winning hand. "My dear, we'll never want for funds," he said to precious Pet. "We'll both be wearing diamonds on all our fingers yet." His patched-up pants lay on the bed resembling bulging bags. "Cut off the buttons, Dear," he said, "and use that trash for rags."

The market seesawed up and down in its accustomed ways. First came a smile and then a frown until those fatal days, when stock quotations gaily slid till margins failed to hold, till Wall Street Bears had clamped the lid upon the Bullies bold, and that's the time when Farmer Jones, with wrinkles on his brow and fast emitting frenzied groans, besought his anxious Frau and said with solemn acumen while venturing a glance, "Please sew those buttons on again, you know, those patched-up pants."

The moral of this little talk should care and caution spread. Don't count your chickens while a hawk is sailing overhead. Don't figure up your income tax while talking to a yegg. Don't think 'neath every duck that quacks you'll find a golden egg.

STONE WALLS

The old wooden fences which cluttered our farm
Were constantly causing us grievous alarm.

With malice intent, without reason or rhyme,
They'd seem to collapse at our busiest time.
Our cattle would ramble all over the place.
We'd spend precious hours in a rodeo chase.
And so, once again, at no major expense,
With axes and spikes we'd patch up that old fence.

But, quite a while later, as wisdom prevailed
And love for stray cattle decidedly paled,
We drew in the rocks from each tillable field,
Which smoothed out the surface and aided the yield.
We piled up those rocks with precision and tact
On row after row till our stamina cracked.
But when we'd completed the task we had planned,
A stone wall encircled the whole of our land.

Our four-footed creatures then grazed where they should,
Hemmed in by stone walls not constructed from wood.
Our neighbors were friendly; no longer they'd groan,
Condemning our cows when they'd call on the phone.
Our families worship those ponderous walls,
Regardless of careless occasional falls,
As our children and intimates enter their claims
For the tops of those walls for their juvenile games.

I sit here refreshed by the bountiful breeze
Made cool by the leaves on our tall, maple trees.
With nostalgic fervor my mem'ry recalls
The labor and love intertwined in those walls.
Those walls are a fixture. They're there for all time
To guard our possessions, for children to climb.
No modernized fencing could ever atone
For those durable monuments fashioned from stone.

THE STORK

Our valleys and vales and our mountains and dales
    Are teeming with birdlife galore.
By brookside and glen, the robin and wren
    Are trilling their songs o'er and o'er.
We list to the lay of the junket and jay,
    And hear the shrill call of the hawk,
But the stork is the best and by everyone blest,
    As he broadcasts his queer little squawk.

He swoops through the air in foul weather or fair,
    And drops without warning at all.

Where'er he alights on his numerous flights,
    We feel the effects of his call.
It's hurry and rush and then silence and hush.
    No longer our lives are serene.
Our much-needed rest is a joke and a jest,
    Since the stork hovered over the scene.

We love all the notes from the wonderful throats
    Of our songsters wherever they're sung.
We delight in the quest of each marvelous nest,
    Where the parent birds cradle their young.
We must all do our share for the comfort and care
    Of the many bird friends with us here.
It's a terrible thing what the future would bring,
    If the stork should by chance disappear.

STORY OF THE ARK

A very long, long time ago, so we have all been told,
Wise men predicted that a flood would all this earth enfold.
So Mr. Noah nervous got, and, while it still was dark,
Decided on the morrow, he would build a monstrous Ark.
So Noah told his wife and sons, while sitting by the fire,
That death from drowning didn't hold for him a great desire,
That in the morning they would build, Shem, Ham, and Japheth all,
A sturdy boat of wondrous size, to weather any squall.
So, putting out the cat and dog and incandescent light,
They climbed the stairs and went to bed, to pass a restless night.
When morning came they early rose and fed the cows and mules,
And after breakfast started out with saws and sundry tools
To build a ship so staunch and tight, 'twould keep the water out,
Provided such a flood should come as they had heard about.
Now when this monster boat was done, they promptly went aboard,
While Noah on the upper deck ope'd wide his mouth and roared:
"Go get a pair of everything that flies and crawls and walks;
Bring porcupines and antelopes, and bears and worms and hawks.
Bring me a pair of honeybees, of buzzards, minks and crows,
In fact, a pair of everything that anybody knows;
So if by any chance the Ark should light upon some land,
We'll let the creatures loose again to breed to beat the band."
So day by day and night by night, in daylight and in dark,
They caught the various animals and put them in the Ark.
They brought the bugs and reptiles and the birds upon the wing,
And finally they had a pair of every living thing.

And when the rain began to come, they closed the bulkhead door
And started out on such a trip as never'd been before.
The rain came down, the Ark went up, how far they didn't know.
The H.C.L. was raising Cain; the food was getting low.
Old Mr. Noah had a job to keep the crocodile
From eating up the mother skunk. His appetite was vile.
And when the lulubird hopped down and got a stranglehold
Upon the father angleworm, then Noah's blood ran cold.
He pounced upon that lulubird, and shouted at his wife,
Who came and pried his bill apart, and saved a precious life.
The father skunk and porcupine were not the best of friends.
They wouldn't hobnob face to face, but turned the other ends.
They both backed up, and, when they met, the quills stuck tight and fast;
The father skunk was peeved and gave the porcupine a blast.
It got in porcupinie's eyes. He knew not where to start;
So Mr. Noah had to come and pry the brutes apart.
They had on board two zurligoes, a female and a male.
Each zurligo had eighteen legs, two fins, four ears, one tail.
The walruses and zurligoes were scrapping on the deck.
One walrus rushed a zurligo and grabbed him by the neck.
The zurligo got twisted 'round, and pricked him with his fin,
Which made the walrus bellow. He got mad, and rushing in
He grabbed that poor old zurligo and rolled him in a ball,
And swallowed him with all his legs, fins, ears, and tail and all.
So that left just one zurligo, which ran away to hide.
She wouldn't eat a single thing and finally she died.
So Noah fed her to the seals. They ate with joy and mirth,
And thus, you see, the zurligoes have vanished from the earth.
Soon after that the flood went down, and downward went the Ark.
It lit upon Mount Ararat, while still 'twas very dark.
When morning came they looked around. The waters all were gone.
The bulkhead door was opened wide, just shortly after dawn.
Out came the creatures, two by two, the birds and beasts and worms.
'Twas hard to keep the elephants from stepping on the germs.
But finally they all got out, and Noah did the same,
And so whatever's happened since, why, Noah is to blame!

STRANGE

He always admired pretty ladies,
The Sandras and Sallys and Sadies,
    But he can't, on his life,
    Explain, for a wife
His choice was as homely as Hades.

SWEETEST SONG

Though I recognized its charm
When I bought the Morton farm
Life alone in strange surroundings had its woe.
But I toiled from early morn
Down amongst the waving corn;
My companions were the harrow and the hoe.
As I took my homeward way,
I could hear the scolding jay
And the whippoorwill who never seemed to tire;
But the sweetest song to me,
And 'twas sung without a key,
Was the singing of the kettle on the fire.

As the seasons came and went,
Harvest came with blessings sent,
For I met a girl with virtues rich and rare,
Laughing eyes and rosy cheeks
And a style the artist seeks,
With a wealth of fluffy locks of golden hair.
As I took my homeward way
I could hear the scolding jay
And the whippoorwill who never seemed to tire;
But the sweetest song to me,
And 'twas sung in faultless key,
Was the singing of my wife before the fire.

Oh, the bliss of wedded life
With a charming, loving wife!
We were happy from the moment we were wed.
Soon those little blessings came,
Vital parts of Cupid's game,
And without them much is lost and love is dead.
As I take my homeward way,
I can hear the scolding jay
And the whippoorwill who never seems to tire;
But the sweetest song to me,
And it's sung in varied key,
Is the song of wife and kiddies by the fire.

SWEETHEART

Oh, what a thrill comes over me,
My memory seems to glow,

As I look backward on a friend
	I knew so long ago.

The years have swiftly passed away,
	But sweetest thoughts remain.
WHAT WOULD I GIVE to just once more
	Caress that form again?

Those arms as smooth as polished wax,
	I fain would touch once more.
And, oh, such legs. I wish that I
	Might see them as of yore.

I don't know what I'd give, again,
	To stroke that jet-black hair.
I'll never have another like
	My favorite old armchair.

SYMPATHETIC MOTHER

"Don't cry, little girl; don't cry.
Perhaps he will come by and by.
It's only three hours you have waited, my dear;
You know I don't think that he's really sincere.
I shouldn't feel sad if he waited a year.
	Don't cry, little girl; don't cry."

"Don't cry, little girl; don't cry.
Perhaps he will come by and by.
How fast he was driving there's no way to tell.
He's probably pinched and is now in a cell.
If he gets what I wish, he'll be there quite a spell.
	Don't cry, little girl; don't cry."

"Don't cry, little girl; don't cry.
Perhaps he will come by and by.
But maybe he's mangled and dead in the wreck,
With a palm in his hand and tire 'round his neck.
	Don't cry, little girl; don't cry."

"Don't cry, little girl; don't cry.
Perhaps he will come by and by.
You know very well he's a numbskull or worse,
And that speedster of his is a terrible curse.
Thank God he can't drive when he rides in the hearse.
	Don't cry, little girl—Oh, hell! Here he comes now!"

SYMPATHY

Oh, Ocean, how my heart goes out to thee.
Cooped up, held fast, thy life is far from free.
Tucked in on every side by rocks and dirt,
Thy bed is so uneven it must hurt.

Through myriad ages thou has been confined,
But, still, as compensation to thy mind
Thy arms are pillowed by receptive sands;
Thy fingers feel the pulse of friendly lands.

Thy heaving bosom flows and ebbs the tide.
This feat must give to thee great joy and pride.
Although thy virtues gloriously shine,
Thy way of life must be, indeed, supine.

Oh, Island, all my sympathies are thine.
Hemmed in on every side by ocean brine
And fettered firmly by terrestrial ties,
'Twould seem impossible for thee to rise.

Thy head and shoulders feel the sun, and yet,
With lower parts perpetually wet,
Discomfort must be thine. How well 'twouldst be
Couldst thou but rise above the soggy sea.

Perchance a jolly earthquake passed thy way,
Inviting thee to join him in his play,
Thy fetters might be loosed, to set thee free,
Or, plunge thy soul into eternity.

With due respect, my sympathies confessing,
The ocean and the island have my blessing;
But, when I die, I trust, in my promotion,
I shall not be an island or an ocean.

TABLETS

Old Dave, overweight and exceedingly fat,
Took tablets for this and the other and that.
But the tablet designed to commemorate Dave
Was the headstone installed at the head of his grave.

The tablets within him continued to work,
And his headstone assumed a mysterious jerk.
Now many a tablet went into that grave,
But the female ones finally quieted Dave.

TALE OF A CAT

A composition is a thing
Not everyone can write.
I never wrote a good one,
Tho I've tried with all my might.

But since my teacher still insists,
That I my part shall do,
I have a tale about a cat
That I'll relate to you.

On a village street not long ago,
There lived a famous cat.
She hardly ever caught a mouse,
And never caught a rat.

She never went to bed till twelve,
And didn't rise till eight.
She used to spend her evenings
Upon her master's gate.

She never sat there all alone,
For every night at nine,
There's forty cats come round to hear
This cat sing "Auld Lang Syne."

She always sang soprano,
While the rest with might and main,
In tenor, bass, and double bass
Joined in the sweet refrain.

Now when three dozen cats, or more,
The same tune try to sing,
The music is so charming
That it never fails to bring

A dozen bootjacks, scores of boots,
Of which the cats have dread,
A half a dozen chunks of coal,
And often chunks of lead.

As soon as such a thing occurs,
As I just now have said,
The cats begin to think 'tis time
That they were all in bed.

So one by one they leave the fence,
And home with footsteps light,
They make their way, all planning
For another just such night.

TENNESSEE TECHNIQUE

Morency Meekus had a farm and most of it was swale.
Although he labored faithfully his crops would always fail.
When springtime floods receded he would work with greatest haste,
But everything he tried to raise would have a muddy taste.
His land was so extremely wet that farming was no fun.
A thousand pounds of any crop would weigh at least a ton.
His soggy squash and cantaloupes, before they reached their prime,
Would float until they weighed enough, then sink beneath the slime.

One day a gentleman rode by and stopped to have a chat.
Said he, "You can't be prosperous by tilling land like that;
Still, there is something you can do and lead a life of ease.
Just fertilize that mud and plant a million rubber trees.
The swamps along the Amazon from Para to the sea
Are similar to those you own right here in Tennessee.
If you will set out rubber plants and nurture them with care,
Some morning you'll jump out of bed a multi-millionaire."

The gentleman beside him wasn't fashioned like a crook.
Morency Meekus rubbed his eyes and took another look.
He thanked his welcome visitor and said with deep regret,
"I wish you had arrived before, but now I'm glad we met."
That afternoon Morency sent a cable to Brazil:
"Ship up a million rubber plants and forward me the bill,"
And then he hastened to his bank with confidence supreme.
He felt he'd need a little help to finance such a scheme.

He met a smiling teller first who welcomed him with glee
But said, "Our credit wizard is the gentleman to see."
Morency in the wizard's lair observed in accents low,
"I've bought a million rubber plants and need a bunch of dough."
The credit wizard blew his nose and calmly scratched his head.
He filled his lungs with Nashville air and seriously said,
"With rubber from a million trees to guarantee a loan,
We probably might stretch a point where friendliness is shown."

Morency Meekus hastened home with gladness in his heart.
He calmly thought things over and decided he was smart.
With greatest tact he managed to repress a joyous shout.

He'd be a multi-millionaire without the slightest doubt.
At last the sprouts began to come by barrel, crate, and case.
He had no thought a million plants would take up so much space.
And then he heard his wifey's voice in accents low and deep,
"Wake up, Morency Meekus, you are talking in your sleep."

TEST OF STRENGTH

The animals came to the shore of the Nile to see who the stronger might be. They came down the valley for many a mile, from mountain and meadow and lea. And when they'd assembled, the creatures, by turns, performed their most difficult stunts. They trampled the weeds and the grasses and ferns, and made the most horrible grunts. The jumping came first and so everyone tried to jump just as far as he could. Some creatures jumped high and some others jumped wide, and landed way out in the wood. The slim ones could jump like the very Old Nick. Their legs seemed to spring like a ball, but the fat ones soon found that their legs were so thick, they hardly were jumping at all. The surly old lion stepped up to the line, and jumped as he'd ne'er jumped before. The creatures all shouted and said it was fine, and marked down his jump on the score. Then came the long tiger, all striped and thin. He placed his big toes on the tape, and jumped with such force he jumped out of his skin, which left him in terrible shape. The leopard then came and got ready to jump. He squatted—then sailed through the air. He lit in the brush with a horrible thump. They looked but no leopard was there. The next one to jump was the bold kangaroo. He smiled as he stepped to the place. His spring was so great that his legs broke in two, and they rolled him away in disgrace. The elephant thought that to jump was a cinch, so he waddled out waving his trunk. He straddled and spraddled and jumped just an inch, and tipped over sideways, kerplunk. Then came the old bear with the grizzly hide. He was roly-and-poly and fat. He couldn't jump straight; so he jumped to one side, and knocked the poor jack-rabbit flat. And now the old crocodile, slim as a rail, to make a big jump then arose, but all he could do was to wobble his tail, and scatter the dirt with his toes. The slimy old "gator" then said that he knew he could trim the old crocodile slick, but to slide on his stomach was all he could do; so they battered his bean with a brick. Ah! Now came the zebra with tail like a whip. He stepped to the line for his jump, but he bent down so low that he stepped on his lip, and down he came crashing, kerplump. The rest of the creatures the jumping game played, but something went wrong all the while, and so they decided to sit in the shade, on the beautiful banks of the Nile. They sat in the shadows till somebody said they would find out the strongest one there, and the old hippopotamus stood on his head and waved his hind legs in the air. The elephant snorted and pulled up a tree, and the lion then bit it in two. The rhinoceros ate up the branches with glee, and the beaver went chewy-chew-chew. They all did their stunts and at last the old skunk stepped out from among all the rest. Said he, "When it comes to the strongest, you're punk, for I am the strongest and best." The creatures all shouted, "Just hear that old guy. Now what does he think he can do?" But the skunk whisked his tail and then winked his left eye, and then he did something else, too. The creatures all watched Mr. Skunk whisk his tail, and laughed to themselves all the while, and then they began to grow steadily pale, with a frown taking place of a smile. They sniffed and they snorted. They really were scared. They never had smelled such a breeze. "He's stronger than we are," the creatures declared, as they scampered away through the trees.

THEY SAY I'M EIGHTY-FIVE

I don't believe I'm eighty-five;
    The record must be lacking.
The fact that I am still alive
    Proves nothing without backing.

If I in eighteen-seventy-two
    Maneuvered my invasion,
I'm wondering, now, exactly who
    Recorded *that* occasion.

I'm not prepared to acquiesce
    And stamp that date's admission.
The way I feel, I must confess
    I'm bounding with ambition.

I have not cashed in all my checks;
    I still know how to figure,
And I adore the sweeter sex
    With undiminished vigor.

I've loved the dearest, sweetest wife
    Through fair and stormy weather.
She's been the treasure of my life,
    Since we have been together.

Our children rank the very best
    With intellects expanding,
Because their mother had been blest
    With love and understanding.

And now, our children's children, too,
    Of varying traits and ages,
Comprise a most delightful crew,
    Our future seers and sages.

I can't believe I'm eighty-five.
    For fame I'm still competing.
I'll strive until my final dive,
    Where Satan does the greeting,

Unless I join the grand parade
    Where saints and angels mingle,
And where I'll need no hearing-aid
    For the soft, celestial jingle.

THIS IS HOW IT HAPPENED

Josephus Jones and Mrs. Jones in solemn silence sat.
No knitting needles clicked apace, no low and friendly chat.
Dark omens for the future filled the cozy place with gloom.
Despondency and hopelessness prevailed throughout the room.

Josephus Jones had lost his job, Depression's deadly toll,
The tiny nest egg in the bank no longer safe and whole.
The stricken woman roused herself and forced a wistful smile.
Her husband kissed her lips and said, "I'm going to walk awhile."

Josephus Jones took up the trail that led through countryside.
By giant trees he worked his way, despondency his guide.
At last, fatigued and out of breath, he paused beside a rill
And, gazing skyward, feebly gasped, "I will! By Heaven, I will!"

Josephus Jones retraced his steps. The way seemed longer now.
Large beads of perspiration coursed down his wrinkled brow.
He plodded on through tangled growth, through brushland up and
    down.
With grim resolve to falter not he made his way to town.

Josephus Jones, with collar up, still lower pulled his cap.
His eyes alone could now be seen within this tiny gap.
He felt that recognition now would be at least remote,
So, darting through a doorway, cast a Democratic vote.

THOUGHTS (UNFINISHED)

The notion that all guns are safe
    Has often been exploded;
A ship which isn't sent away
    Will never come back loaded.

The man who has a leaky purse
    With no desire to mend it
Can only expect poverty
    And wait for death to end it.

The foolish cat who falls asleep,
    His feline vigil shirking,
Won't catch the rat who keeps awake
    With all his talents working.

THWARTED

When comes my finish, by and by,
As I lie down and calmly die,
    The sundry germs
    And crawling worms
Will really be elated.
They'll come from south, west, north, and east
To share the tender, juicy feast.
    But here's a tip:
    Their plans will slip—
I'm going to be cremated.

TIME

Old Father Time has made a perfect score.
With stealthy tread he hastens to our door
And lingers not for leave to enter in,
But stalks across our threshold with a grin.
His presence spreads a chill all roundabout;
We all in turn desire to kick him out.
We thump our chests and ape the springy step
To show him that we still are blest with pep.

But Father Time knows better. All the signs—
The stooping shoulders and the telltale lines
That he has deftly placed, we all may see
Deep wrinkles now where smoothness used to be;
Where once the cheek of childhood wore a blush,
Today stiff whiskers bristle like a brush;
Where once the golden tresses fair had been,
Today the contrast shows them gray and thin.

Yes, Time has power beyond all human ken;
His heavy footsteps crush the will of men.
Still, those who battle well against his might
May stem the fatal day—prolong the fight.
Have courage! Do not cringe from Father Time,
Advancing with his scythe besmirched with grime,
Nor cast aside with condescending bow
The golden opportunities of Now.

TO MR. STALIN

You may think you're God Almighty, but we know
That you're a sham, and your boasted five-year
Planning won't be worth a tinker's dam, and
You'll rate a small "I used to be," instead of
Great "I AM," for the cards are stacked against
You, Mr. Stalin.

You would wipe out human progress which would
Not return for years. You would murder precious
Manhood; you would squander human tears, but you'll
Lean against the chilly fact a wrench is in the
Gears, for the World will be against you, Mr. Stalin.

If you only knew what's coming you would hide
Your head in shame, for your foes have only
Started, but they'll get there just the same. And
Your poor, misguided nation will be very glad they
Came, for your people are against you, Mr. Stalin.

When the devil sees you coming at the end of
Your career, with a shudder he'll address you with
A warning crisp and clear, "Yours will be our first
Refusal, for you're quite unwelcome here." Even Hell
Will be against you, Mr. Stalin.

TOBACCO

Oh, my! Certain people propose to abolish
The use of tobacco in every known form.
We smokers must rise in our wrath and demolish
Such crazy desire, in a protesting storm.
It's hard to conceive how a bunch of crusaders
Can squander their time in a manner so dumb.
Their equipment is perfect for teaching first-graders.
No nourishment follows from sucking the thumb.

How sad it would be to arise some fine morning
To find that the pipe and cigars were tabooed.
Poor wife would discover without any warning
That hubby was not in his usual mood.
The dear, darling kiddies would cleverly scatter.
The cat in the corner would beat it from there,
And the cook nimbly stirring the griddlecake batter
Would hurl the whole works at the burly old bear.

Some people believe that to smoke is a menace
That leads a man toward the sarcophagus latch,
And others declare that in water-soaked Venice
Alone there's no danger from lighting a match.
The nicotine feature they're unduly stressing.
Physicians indulge and they're hearty and hale.
The cigar or the pipe is a wonderful blessing.
To ban them won't cause any wavering wail.

TREES

When in solitude I ponder
Nature's masterpieces yonder,
'Tis the forest that engenders inspiration in my soul.
No inanimate creations
Bring to me profound sensations
Like a densely wooded valley or a timber-crested knoll.

Oh, I know that lofty mountains
And the weird volcano fountains,
Rushing rivers, massive glaciers, are devotedly sublime,
But to me the most alluring
And forever reassuring,
Is the growth of forest timber till the very end of time.

212

Here the sunshine and the weather
Work their miracles together
That the forest in its splendor may survive till Judgment Day.
Here the timid forest creatures
Find contentment in the features
Of their solitary fortress where their young can safely play.

Trees enhance mankind's devotion;
Fill our minds with deep emotion,
If perchance we have the vision to appreciate their worth.
Forest growth alone can save us,
All the soil that Nature gave us.
Trees are one of God's creations. Save the trees and save the Earth.

TRUE LOVE

Wait till the moonlight shines upon the water,
    Then take your sweetheart out for a spin.
Mind what I say, boys; that's the way to court her—
    Tell her you will wed her when your ship comes in.
Snuggle her and squeeze her; tickle her and tease her.
    Tell her lots of little fibs, saying they are true.
Mind what I say, boys; that's the way to please her—
    Tell her you will wed her if she'll wait for you.

Don't keep her anxious; take her out to dinner.
    Don't keep her waiting; take her out tonight.
Mind what I say, boys; that's the way to win her—
    Tell her you will wed her in the fireflies' light.
Fondle her, caress her, praise her to impress her.
    Tell her she is lovely as a fairy fay.
Mind what I say, boys; bluff her well and bless her—
    Tell her you will wed her on her wedding day.

Give her proof you're able to support her;
    Tell her of your rich old uncle Bill.
Mind what I say, boys; that's the way to court her.
    Tell her you will wed her when they read the will.
Demonstrate your dander, corral her and brand her.
    Tell her she is lucky with a guy like you.
Mind what I say, boys; that's the way to land her—
    Tell her you will wed her and be sure you do.

213

TWO BOYS

While out upon my daily stroll I entered Crescent Park.
The pond was frozen over but the ice was thin and dark.
I knew the surface wasn't safe on which to trust a skate.
Two youngsters stood with skates in hand, bemoaning cruel fate.

One boy was dressed in costly garb. A rich man's son was he.
I marveled at his cultured talk and sparkling repartee.
The other lacked these finer points. The contrast was complete.
His clothing barely camouflaged this urchin of the street.

I started conversation by remarking, "This is great,
To have a pond so near to town, but aren't you going to skate?"
The favored son removed his cap and brightly answered, "No,
I sadly fear submergence in congealing H_2O."

I then addressed the other lad who slyly gazed at me.
Said I, "My boy, have you the same presentiment as he?"
He thought a moment then a grin upon his face appeared,
And chuckling to himself replied, "Oh, no, I'm on'y skeered."

UNCLE JOE'S DIVINING ROD

The mystical divining rod, that crotched witch hazel bough,
Has baffled men of ancient times and baffles men right now.
In fact, at present, many men, the whole wide world around,
Admit its power to find a stream that flows far underground.

In Jacksonville there lived a man well versed in magic things.
For seventy years he'd spent his time in seeking hidden springs.
He'd walk across a certain spot, witch hazel crotch in hand,
And when it dipped they always found pure water in the sand.

Suppose a man in Idaho desired to dig a well.
He'd send at once for Uncle Joe and he would come pell-mell.
He'd strut around upon the vale and grasp his magic wand,
And like as not discover juice enough to make a pond.

One time he took a northern trip and later, homeward bound,
On reaching Kansas stopped awhile to take a look around.
He hunted up some ancient pals and they, of long ago,
Decided on a little joke to play on Uncle Joe.

They knew their old-time friend possessed a vast amount of pride.
They knew that his witch hazel fame had traveled far and wide,
And on a broad expanse of swale they subtly laid their plan,
Where fifteen feet beneath the ground the giant sewer ran.

So Uncle Joe was taken on a wide inspection tour.
They said they hoped he'd find a spring of water, clear and pure.
And Uncle Joe, supposed to be the world's most famous seer,
Of course would ferret out a source of water, pure and clear.

The telephones worked overtime and thus the message sped,
And rumors of a miracle around the county spread.
A crowd of many thousand souls assembled there to watch
This clever man manipulate his weird witch hazel crotch.

Then Uncle Joe rolled up his sleeves and in the sunshine basked.
"Ye'd like to find fresh water here. Is that the game?" he asked.
"Yes, that's the game," the echo came. The crowd pressed closer now,
As Uncle Joe untied a string that held his hazel bough.

His calloused hands now firmly grasped the magic hazel limb.
He slowly aimed the lower prongs waist high in front of him.
The crotch above remained erect and trembled slightly there,
As Uncle Joe advanced a step with concentrated care.

Then step by step he made his way across the grassy slope.
His eyes were on the hazel bough. His heart was filled with hope.
The thousands who were gathered there were keyed to highest pitch,
When suddenly the hazel bough began to jerk and twitch.

It yanked and twisted, pulled and hauled, and nearly burst in twain.
The massive hands controlling it were trembling from the strain.
He lost his grip upon the prongs, his fingers dripping blood,
And Uncle Joe, bewildered, faint, collapsed with heavy thud.

The magic wand, unhampered, jumped about as if possessed.
The very last they saw of it, it vanished rolling west.
Said Uncle Joe, "Here, help me up," and added with a groan;
"I never felt such hellish power. Oh, where's a telephone?"

They bandaged up his bleeding hands and to the city sped.
The car which carried Uncle Joe a grand procession led.
They climbed the steps and Uncle Joe, disheveled, grim and tanned,
Addressed the operator there with a severe command.

"Gimme the mayor of Jacksonville, as speedy as ye can."
The buzzers buzzed. The girl replied, "Well, mister, here's your man."
Then Uncle Joe took up the phone and yelled with all his might,
"The Gulf Stream's under Kansas State. Is Floridy all right?"

UNDER THE RAFTERS

Underneath the attic rafters sat a white-and-yellow cat
That apparently intently gazed upon a monstrous rat
That supposedly envisioned what appeared in store for him,
If perchance the cat decided to devour him, limb by limb.

Not a twitching of a whisker disarranged the attic air,
And the pussy's tail, extended, harbored not a ruffled hair.
And the rat remained so quiet that the silence was intense,
Which would indicate the fellow lacked his share of common sense.

Thus they savored one another in a most amazing way.
Each displayed no inclination for indulging in a fray.
Neither moved a tiny muscle. Neither winked a troubled eye.
One afraid? The other timid? What a crazy alibi.

Could the cat have been so sleepy that he couldn't smell a rat?
Could the rat have been so silly that he didn't fear a cat?
Would it aid your understanding if a message came to you
That the rat was made of cotton and the cat was cotton, too?

UP HERE

My gun is on my shoulder and my shells are in my bag.
I hope Saint Peter doesn't kick if I should shoot a stag.
The hunting here is easier than down in U.S.A.,
No fallen trees or bramble briars forever in the way.

No hunting dogs are here allowed to track the nimble deer;
Sweet female angels take their place and do the chasing here.
With female grace and perfect ease they leap the silver rills
And glide around among the ferns and golden daffodils.

A lovely angel flapped her wings and sidled up to me.
She took my arm and led me underneath a tulip tree.
She motioned me to take a seat upon the golden grass
And sitting down beside me said, "I am a lonely lass."

Perhaps I should not mention this, but what was I to do?
I had some second thoughts, but snuggled PDQ!
I don't recall what happened underneath that tulip tree,
But hunting was the leastest thing that interested me.

VACCINATION

Since vaccination made its bow
    To scientific men,
Much praise it's had from then till now
    With censure now and then.
But records show a dread disease
    So fatal to mankind
Can now be warded off with ease,
    But there's a scar, we find.

A scar that ladies, old and young,
    Desire to have concealed.
They'd much prefer to lose a lung
    Than have that scar revealed.
And so, at first, a sleeve they'd raise
    And take it on the arm,
A method that deserved much praise,
    Dispelling all alarm.

But changing styles in spring and fall
    Spread havoc near and far.
First, shorter sleeves, then none at all
    Disclosed that fearful scar.
The debutantes were sorely pressed.
    Dark visions filled the mind.
No space they found when fully dressed
    In front nor yet behind.

But woman's ingenuity
    Had never met defeat,
And science's perpetuity
    Remained on easy street.
The gentler sex was duly stirred
    By inspiration's dare;
A darkened room, a whispered word,
    The doctor put it there.

And, though that dreaded telltale spot
    Today is well obscured,
Continuance, as like as not,
    Can scarcely be assured,
Because the modern styles in dress
    Are changing day by day.
What's coming is an outside guess,
    As seasons slip away.

But science deftly wins again
    And here the secret lies;
They've found a spot on maids and men
    Immune from spying eyes,
The last resort the fashion sharks
    Are likely to infest.
Our future vaccination marks—
    Or maybe you have guessed.

VIEWPOINT

The baby came in course of time as babies always do.
He had a dimple in his cheek and lovely eyes of blue.
His chubby fists were doubled up in pugilistic style.
"We'll call him 'Samson,'" said papa. "Oh, look, just see him smile!"

Dear mother showed no interest while father rambled on.
He dropped the name of "Samson" for the simple name of "John."
But keen deliberation made him change the name once more.
He thought of "Teddy Roosevelt" and favored "Theodore."

But "Solomon" and "Socrates," "Pythagoras" and "Paul";
"Hippocrates" and "Hannibal," and "Cicero" and "Saul";
"Hercules," "Herodotus," "Joshua" and "James";
"Antony" and "Abraham" were such appealing names,

Then daddy paused, and pondered that perhaps it might be fair
To counsel wifey when a name be chosen for the heir.
Poor mother hadn't said one word, but still possessed her wits.
She weakly whispered to the nurse, "We're going to call it quits."

VITAMINS

I never have witnessed in all of my days
A thing so unique as this vitamin craze.
How man has progressed to his present degree
Without vitamin knowledge is far beyond me.
But I've noticed some changes in people I know,
Since this vitamin slant has been stealing the show.
Folks seem to possess what they formerly lacked,
With their minds more at ease being logical fact.

Old Ezra DeLong was decrepit and lame,
But after the vitamins entered his frame,
He scampered about like a thoroughbred steer;
You'd think he had blended his whiskey and beer.
His wife was alarmed at the way he behaved.
He smelled of cologne and twice daily he shaved.
His appetite strengthened beyond all belief;
For all of his meals he craved red-blooded beef.

Bill Coe for a while was enduringly tired.
He lacked nearly everything vigor required,
But after partaking of vitamin X
His actions appealed to the feminine sex.
They sought and pursued him which gave him a thrill.
For a time he denied them with masculine skill.
At last he got hooked and he's now signing checks
To replenish his vanishing vitamin X.

Now, there's Newman Shaw, an adorable man.
He couldn't eat anything stronger than bran,
But he swallowed some capsules of vitamin L,
And look at him now; he's as husky as anything.
And Artie Montgomery used to be slim,
But vitamins caused rapid changes in him.
I'm sure if he eats a few vitamins more,
He will be quite unable to walk through the door.

Bert Winters took vitamin K by the crate.
He thought they would give him the vigor to skate,
But his blood got so hot the ice melted away;
Still, his wife is all praises for vitamin K.
Pat Snead has a cow that refused to produce;
So he fed her six doses of vitamin juice.
The cow then responding with vigor and grace,
Had beautiful twins with a V on each face.

This vitamin game will stay with us, I'm sure.
They'll probably cause a remarkable cure
For those who imagine their ills are severe,
While daily expecting their finish is near.
So let's be resigned to this vitamin splurge.
Perhaps from disaster we all may emerge.
Perhaps we'll have nothing but genuine praise
For this incomprehensible vitamin craze.

VOLSTEAD ACT

The dipper in the milky-way
    With milk was filled each minute.
Then came the Volstead Act one day.
    Since then, there's moonshine in it.
And when the dipper overflowed
    With milk, it seldom found us,
But with a moonshine overload,
    It splashes all around us.

WAITING

I've spent my lifetime waiting for the mail.
I've waited for the passing of the gale.
I've waited for the telephone to ring.
I've waited for the fall and for the spring.

I've waited in the sunshine and the shade.
I've waited for my book to make the grade.
I've waited for the checks to come along,
For articles I've written, verse and song.

I've waited for a letter, long o'erdue,
From Protestant or Catholic or Jew.
I've waited for the coming of the rain
To save the crops, and oftentimes in vain.

I've spent much time in waiting, I confess,
But still I'm not alone in my distress.
My Old Maid friends are hot upon the trail.
They also have been waiting for the male.

A WARNING

The little red schoolhouse is only a dream,
A dream Joe will never forget.
He loved every shingle and clapboard and beam,
From the basement below to the jet.
He knew all the cracks which admitted the breeze
Through November to March every year
And how they'd thaw out from their shivers and freeze
By the pot-bellied stove in the rear.

Joe knew every boy and he knew every girl.
He still can remember them now.
His mind wanders back to a cute little curl
Which adorned a particular brow.
He thought at the time that no lovelier lass
Ever smiled at a boy in distress.
When they played drop-the-handkerchief out on the grass,
Where he dropped it you'll probably guess.

But time had the habit of changing the rule
Which applied to all feminine grace.
In time other lassies attended that school;
Newcomers invaded the place.
Joe, sizing things up with a critical eye,
Beheld some new angles in charm.
He promptly imagined he couldn't see why
Postponement could do any harm.

Throughout his whole life Joe has favored that view.
Decisions to him were a joke.
Bald-headed and gray he is now eighty-two,
Unmarried, unpopular, broke.
He sits on a stump by the side of the road,
Despondent, remorseful, alone.
With candid repugnance he watches a toad,
Whose virtues outnumber his own.

WATER

Ben used to be from trouble free; no aches or pains he carried. He'd take a whack at applejack in barrooms where he tarried. He always took his whiskey clear and chased it down with lager beer and kept it up year after year, until the time he married.

Then all was changed. His wife arranged a very different system. His pal came 'round and with a bound she rushed outside and hissed him. "You needn't wander here," she said. "I'll on your Adam's apple tread." She shied a brickbat at his head which very barely missed him.

He now perceived that she was peeved that he'd have such a crony. He had a task to hide his mask and prove he wasn't phony. But as the years went slipping by, she weaned him from the rock and rye, and he became a decent guy and people called him Toney.

And then, altho 'twas long ago he used to take a nipper, and on a bun would always shun the sparkling water dipper, the time came 'round when he could feel depression from a hearty meal, while 'round and 'round his head would reel, and he was far from chipper.

His darling wife then saved his life, altho his symptoms grieved her. She knew right well his ailing spell was caused by rum, which peeved her. "Drink naught but rippling water, Ben, and you will soon be well again." And he replied, "I'll try it, Jen," altho he disbelieved her.

It's hard to say what time of day he started water sipping. At any rate, it wasn't late, he saw the ceiling tipping. The room whirled 'round and roundabout, which turned his insides inside out. In water's virtues he'd a doubt; he felt his courage slipping.

But Jen declared she wasn't scared to with the water soak him, and when he'd yell like merry Ned she'd pour it down and choke him. He swallowed water by the kegs, till now his frame insists and begs that he shall even lap its dregs, but from the booze it broke him.

He says right now his darling frau is glad she isn't single. His every step is full of pep. His jeans with shekels jingle. The luscious water did the trick. If you who read these lines are sick, just drink a barrel mighty quick and with the huskies mingle.

WAY DOWN SOUTH

My heart am sad an' lonely an' my eyes am growin' dim;
    I'm listenin' now for Gabriel's horn to blow.
I am waitin' for de message dat will surely come from Him,
    Who is watchin' for de endin' of my row.
De times has changed most wondrous for de young folks of today;
    No mo dey likes to gather roun' my do',
But dey listens when de autos come to tote 'em all away,
    An' I miss 'em ebery minute, mo' an' mo'.

Oh, give me back de good old days when I was young an' gay;
    Oh, give me back dose times I loved so well,
When de young folks would be gatherin' at de closin' of de day
    For to hear de stories dat I used to tell.

I'm sittin' here an' thinkin' of de days when I was young,
    When dancers came a-waltzin' to an' fro.
I can hear again de hummin' as de cabin songs were sung
    An' I picked de music from de ol' ban-jo.

But everythin' is changin' now from what it used to be;
    No mo' dey comes a-rompin' when I call,
For de pictures an' de radio are mo' delight dan me,
    An' de banjo hangs a-danglin' on de wall.

Oh, bring me back dem joyous hours to brighten up de way.
    Oh, change my evenin' shadows into dawn.
An' again I'll be a-workin' an' a-singin' all de day
    Out amongst de wavin' cotton an' de cawn.

I'm thinkin' of de time when I shall climb de Golden Stair
    An' leave behind my trouble an' my woe.
I desires de au-to-mo-bile an' de radio won't be dere
    For to keep de bredren always on de go.
No mo' I'll think of sadness in de Savior's Home above,
    Where everyone am equal in His sight,
Where de Angels preach de Gospel in de ways of truth an' love,
    Where no darkness ever dims de Heavenly Light.

Oh, give me peace an' quiet in dat far-off Promised Land;
    No reason for to sorrow an' to weep,
Wid de music flowin' peaceful from dat blessed Angel band,
    For I's tired an' I wants to go to sleep.

WE COME THIS WAY BUT ONCE

We come this way but once, my friend,
    Then leave the scene behind.
So why not, ere the journey's end,
    Do something for mankind?

High-sounding words have never laid
    Foundation stones in line,
And conversation never made
    A temple or a shrine.

Fine phrases never formed a wall,
    Nor built a lovely tower,
And all the words you may recall
    Can't grow a gorgeous flower.

Though kindly words from me to you
    May benefit mankind,
Exalted deeds are needed, too.
    Let's leave a few behind.

WEATHER BUREAU

The weather bureau gives out tips.
It's sometimes right but often slips
    Concerning weather trends.
It costs enough to be OK.
They tell us when to cut our hay,
    On which success depends.

But often when it mentions "fair,"
We start our mowing over there
    Amongst the honeydew;
And when our hay is nicely dry
A flock of clouds obscures the sky
    And torrents soak it through.

When weather is extremely dry
And crops are short and feed is high,
    We sit and twirl our thumbs,
And listen to the bureau hour,
As it predicts a welcome shower,
    A shower that never comes.

The weather bureau prophesied,
"There'll be a wind and rising tide;
    So gather in the ducks."
The damage from that wind and rain
In the ensuing hurricane—
    Four hundred million bucks.

We raise big squashes by the ton,
And they require much rain and sun,
    As everybody knows.
One night we listened, "Never fear;
No frosty freezes will appear,"
    And all our squashes froze.

So, now, when I desire the truth,
I ask some simple, naive youth,
    "Think you we'll have a freeze?"
He wets his finger in his mouth
And holds it up and says, "It's south;
    No frost tonight, by Jees."

Now when the radio whispers, "Fair,"
We place our raincoats here and there
    All set for safety's sake,

224

And if it mentions frost and snow
Away our heavy duds all go
    And everything is jake.

WHEN THE BUTTERFLIES
ARE TRAVELING IN PAIRS

All the world is full of gladness,
Joy and sunshine, peace and love;
'Tis no time to think of sorrows and of cares.
Singled out from all the rest,
Is the time we love the best
When the butterflies are traveling in pairs.

When the butterflies are traveling in pairs,
Then I meet my darling sweetheart on the stairs;
With her welcome hand in mine we go strolling down the line,
While the butterflies are traveling in pairs.

Now we'll find a shady resting place
Upon a mossy bank,
And my heart with joy o'erflows when she declares:
"Since you've asked me to decide,
I'll be glad to be your bride,
Since the butterflies are traveling in pairs."

Since the butterflies are traveling in pairs,
Here's a ring I hope my darling always wears.
Slip it on your finger tight; it will tie the knot all right,
For the butterflies are traveling in pairs.

Now we'll find a cozy cottage
Nestled in among the hills
Where Dame Nature from her storehouse freely shares;
When the parson says we're one,
Our real lives have just begun,
As the butterflies are traveling in pairs.

When the butterflies are traveling in pairs,
We together now will share our joys and cares.
We have joined the only throng that really drives the world along.
'Tis much better to be traveling in pairs.

WHERE THE PUNCHING BAG HUNG

We boys on the farm in the days long ago
Had pleasures and thrills in a non-ending flow.
The old swimming pool furnished rest from the heat,
And in winter its coating of ice was a treat.
The skating and hockey and coasting the hills,
Snowshoeing and skiing all gave us rare thrills.
But the thoughts of those days that have steadfastly clung
Concerned the old shed where the punching bag hung.
We'd whang it and bang it; we'd knock it and sock it,
And rock that old shed where the punching bag hung.

No boys could have garnered more genuine glee
In youth than befell to my brothers and me.
We never shot birds but the fox was a pest,
And his capture involved a rare marksmanship test.
The strolls through the woodlands, the casting for trout,
The fishing for pickerel, bass, and horned pout
Brought joy to us all, but most praises were sung
For the little old shed where the punching bag hung.
We'd slam it and wham it. We'd paste it and baste it,
And shake that old shed where the punching bag hung.

When work time was over, then one of us led
A rollicking rush to the welcome old shed,
Where the weights and the dumbbells and lifting machine
Produced competition delightfully keen.
We each took a turn at the different stunts
That strengthened our morals and muscles at once.
We'd siphon sweet cider right out through the bung,
In that little old shed where the punching bag hung.
We'd whack it and smack it, and, oh, what a racket
Would come from that shed where the punching bag hung.

It seems only yesterday when as a kid
I tried to outdo what my brothers all did.
As I was some younger, in boxing they won,
But in punching the bag I was seldom outdone.
With a rub-a-dub-dub and a rat-a-tat-tat,
That bag must have wondered just where it was at.
Oh, what would I give once again to be young
And visit that shed where the punching bag hung.
Although you may guess it, I'd fondly caress it,
That precious old shed where the punching bag hung.

WHY WE HAVE CHRISTMAS

Long ago, my mother tells me, in a manger filled with hay,
In a town the Jews called Bethlehem a tiny baby lay.
And his mother watched him tenderly within the manger there,
Always hoping he would sometime be a man of goodness rare.

When he reached the age of manhood all her cherished hopes came true,
As he preached and led his people in a way entirely new,
For he showed them by example truth and love must lead the way,
And his teachings have survived the years down to our present day.

But in that distant period two thousand years ago
Lived wicked men who did not wish the seed of truth to grow.
And so they ridiculed his views and scoffed at what he said,
Then took his life and placed a wreath of thorns upon his head.

But though they killed this godlike man, his teachings still survive,
And upright people follow them as though he were alive.
Throughout the world the name of Christ is known where people pray,
And that is why we gather here to keep this Christmas Day.

WILD CREATURES VIEW MANKIND

The creatures were assembled underneath the spreading trees. They'd come from distant places and enjoyed the cooling breeze. They'd gathered there for arguments concerning world affairs. They wanted solid facts and didn't favor splitting hairs.

The porcupine pulled out a quill and dipped it in the mud, and what he wrote astounded the survivors of the flood. He wrote that Mr. Noah and his married sons and wives had failed to set the standards for all future Christian lives.

The monkey then threw out his chest and waved a monkey arm, and said: "Delinquent juveniles should cause them no alarm. If one of ours should imitate the offspring of the men, we'd slap him down and stand him up and slap him down again."

The elephant responded as he wildly waved his trunk: "Those ultra-modern scientists are just a lot of bunk. The scientific Russians are as crazy as a loon. They claim that they can catapult a rocket to the moon.

"And now the dopes in Yankeeland have fallen into line. A way to spend more money seems a very welcome sign. A billion here, a billion there, and other billions yet will simply add more billions to their mounting national debt."

"You're very right," the lion said and shook his shaggy mane. "It makes me doubly certain that those humans are insane. For heaven's sake, what nincompoop would welcome such a trip? He'd need a bottle in his hand, another on his hip."

The tiger said: "The leaders of the whites and blacks and red should surely be examined for their large but hollow heads. Their sputniks, bombs, and satellites forebode a certain doom, thus leaving every continent immersed in total gloom."

The rabbit, widely heralded the meekest of the fold, then hopped upon a stump and faced the creatures, wild and bold. "I don't know why we linger here; we cannot turn the tide. The human race is destined for collective suicide.

"The only thing they worship is a giant show of might, and one thing they've adopted is the slogan—Might Makes Right! They talk of peace and practice war, which has a rotten smell. I move we now adjourn and let them blow themselves to hell."

WINTERTIME

The old folks tell of old-time winters,
    No snow removal debt.
This winter knocks them all to splinters
    And isn't finished yet.

I well remember drifting blizzards
    Across the roads and walls.
We had no tele-radio wizards
    To warn of coming squalls.

No autos clogged the drains and gutters
    Assembled in a row,
And horses drew the sleighs and cutters
    Atop the well-packed snow.

They tramped it down in solid layers
    To form an icy crust.
No high-priced, arm-chair street surveyors
    Were classified a "must."

Our roads were left in that condition
 (Quite different today),
Until the sun performed its mission
 By melting it away.

But then the autos changed the picture
 And labor needed cash.
The modern road is now a fixture
 For Packard, Ford, or Nash.

But still I'd favor no returning
 To times before the Jeep,
Though I'll admit I have no yearning
 For snowdrifts eight feet deep.

Those older folks by reminiscing
 Degrade the status-quo.
The rest of us rejoice at missing
 An avalanche of snow.

But soon our welcome southern breezes
 Will melt the snow to slush.
We'll miss those atmospheric freezes
 And plow through mud and mush.

Though we condemn the winter season
 In manner grim and terse,
With ample show of rhyme and reason,
 The aftermath is worse.

THE WIZARD

He was the wisest man in seven counties,
And, what is more, he didn't care who knew it.
He solved the problems of the Royal Mounties.
His slogan was, "Get started, then pursue it."

He oft advised the warring Asiatics.
Astronomy had claimed his close attention.
A zealous star in higher mathematics,
He made a monkey of the fourth dimension.

In art he ranked among the foremost critics,
Deploring lack of adequate expression.
His treatise on the cure for paralytics
Enthroned him in the medical profession.

He knew all potent cures for indigestion
And claimed that none surpassed the ancient vichy,
But couldn't handle little daughter's question,
"If your uncle's sister's not your aunt, who is she?"

WOLF

A ravenous wolf, on a foraging tour
Through cottonwood, cedar, and pine,
Stalked hither and yon with intent to secure
A meal of substantial design.

At last, in a clearing, a well-nourished ewe,
Apart from the others, appeared.
The wolf took a highly professional view
And with lamby's desires interfered.

The battle was short but the feasting endured,
Till the wolf like a glutton became,
And shortly thereafter disquiet matured,
Which enveloped the whole of his frame.

A virtuous rabbit, by sympathy stirred,
And awed by his ponderous size,
Consolingly whispered a comforting word.
The wolf groaned and leered in surprise.

"How come?" asked the wolf. "Why this mushy appeal?"
"I'd like to be married," she said.
So by animal rites and the wilderness seal
The wolf and the rabbit were wed.

He greeted his bride with a flattering kiss,
Then led her away to his den,
Where they sojourned awhile in debatable bliss,
Till the wolf became hungry again.

"Come, Pet," said the wolf. "I will give you a hug."
But the rabbit had other designs.
She slid down a hole she had recently dug
And emerged in the blackberry vines.

The wolf settled down on the newly-made hole,
Intending to smother his wife.
The rabbit, secure on the blackberry knoll,
Discovered the chance of her life.

Selecting a thorn from a blackberry bush,
She quickly dove down in the dirt;
Coming up 'neath the wolf, with a muscular push,
She inserted the thorn where it hurt.

The wolf gave a spring and a thunderous roar;
His head struck the top of the lair.
He fell in a murderous rage to the floor;
The rabbit departed from there.

She hurdled the hummocks, while shouting in glee;
She sang as she hurried along,
"Who's afraid of the wolf?" which was destined to be
The theme of a popular song.

WOODCHUCKS

Farmer Palmer hastened home from Palm Beach by the ocean.
His great success with fishworms brought about another notion.
He figured that if fishworms could make business so alluring,
The woodchuck possibilities could be quite reassuring.

He got a hundred woodchucks as a starting operation,
But families of ten or twelve increased the population.
They multiplied a hundredfold and clover was their diet.
He had to increase acreage to keep those woodchucks quiet.

Electric fences kept them in but water was essential,
And sanitation problems were no longer confidential.
The neighbors signed a document protesting noxious odors,
Which could not well associate with drugstore ice-cream sodas.

Now Farmer Palmer knew enough to grasp the situation.
He'd slaughter every woodchuck and retain his reputation.
And then he had a clever thought connected with the fiddle;
If catgut furnished fiddle strings, his woodchucks solved the riddle.

He used a poison chamber so the woodchucks wouldn't suffer.
If catgut made good fiddle strings his product would be tougher.
He hired a bunch of specialists who paid him strict attention,
And how those fiddle strings appeared surpassed all comprehension.

Why violins and mandolins and harpsichords and zithers
Responded to those woodchuck strings had music men in dithers.
The catgut strings were obsolete, the cause for their rejection,
While woodchuck strings brought harmony and musical perfection.

Though Farmer Palmer took no stock in conjurers or witches,
For fifty bucks he'd show a man the shortest road to riches.
He'd whisper in a client's ear some woodchuck words of magic,
And oftentimes the consequence would be extremely tragic.

But still he had his fifty bucks, a cushion for his action,
Which magnified a thousand times enhanced his satisfaction.
And while you folks are reading this authenticated story,
The lowly woodchuck perches on a pedestal of glory.

THE WRECK

When the good ship *Waving Willow*
Sank beneath the ocean billow
Off the coast of Honolulu where Hawaiian music rolls,
Just two passengers were lucky,
And to say that they were plucky
Would be stating it too mildly; they were super-valiant souls.

When the stricken ship upended,
Human ties were rudely rended,
As the suction from the sinking pulled them down and down and down.
All, including Captain Crocker,
Sank to Davy Jones's Locker,
Save the two whom I have mentioned, who decided not to drown.

Lucy Larkin treaded water,
Till Horatius Hanna caught her,
And propelled her to a table that by chance was floating by.
This Miss Lucy deftly straddled,
And Horatius proudly paddled
To the sweetest little island underneath the tropic sky.

"We must hoist a signal banner,"
Said the moist Horatius Hanna.
Lucy wore an inner garment which she disengaged with ease.
From a lush growth, tall and tender,
Came a sapling slimly slender,
And aloft the garment floated on the Honolulu breeze.

"We could count it quite a favor,"
Said Horatius with a quaver,
"If that banner met the vision of the lookout on a yacht."
Then responded dripping Lucy,
"I don't relish feeling juicy.
Let's dry out on yonder hilltop where the solar rays are hot."

So together they ascended
To the point where climbing ended,
To the topmost rocky level where the ocean view was grand.
But Horatius paused to ponder
That the view forever yonder
Was not half so vision-pleasing as the view more close at hand.

Lucy also tired of gazing
At the view, although amazing,
And devoted more attention to the man who saved her life.
As their clothes were slowly drying,
All the rules of form denying,
She addressed Horatius Hanna, "Did you ever have a wife?"

When he answered "No," she listened,
And her eyes with luster glistened,
As she spoke to Mr. Hanna in a most enticing way.
"I am just a modern maiden
With a love for living laden,
And I like it here immensely," and continued then to say,

"There are oyster shells for dishes;
If we catch some finny fishes
We may win a fair subsistence on this lovely tropic isle.
We can snugly work together
In this mild Hawaiian weather,
And we'll soon become acquainted," she insisted with a smile.

Down the signal garment fluttered
And Horatius Hanna stuttered,
"Lu—Lu—Lucy, do you mean it? You have put me on the spot."
But judging by their laughter
They'd be happy ever after,
As the parson-bird alighted just in time to tie the knot.

YES

I know that I shall never hear
A word so welcome to my ear
As when, accepting my caress,
A charming maiden answered, "Yes."

'Twas on a glorious winter day
We nestled in a covered sleigh.
With ecstasy I could not hide,
I asked her if she'd be my bride.

The robes were tucked in snug and tight.
The snow was drifting, pure and white.
Old Jerry didn't seem to care,
If we remained forever there.

I know again I'll never feel
The consciousness of such appeal,
Planned by the Lord that winter day,
Enacted in a covered sleigh.

EPILOGUE

Stand, as the column approaches our station.
Hail, to our Flag at the head of the line.
This is the emblem upholding our nation;
This is the Flag of your country and mine.

This is the Flag that our forefathers cherished
During their struggle for liberty's life.
Certain it is that their cause would have perished
But for that Flag in the turmoil and strife.

This is the Flag that our fathers defended
Valiantly, fearlessly, nobly and well,
Till the great battles for freedom were ended,
Till the secessionists' fortitude fell.

Proudly it waved o'er the nation united;
Proudly it waves o'er our country today.
Calmly and clearly our forebears incited
Plans which would lead us in liberty's way.

Long may this emblem continue to serve us,
Preaching of freedom's great gift to the world.
Long may our liberty live to preserve us
From the dire threats that dictators have hurled.

Stand, as the column approaches our station.
Hail, to our Flag at the head of the line.
Lift up your voices in grand salutation—
Liberty lives for your children and mine.

235